MOROCCO

GREAT LITTLE GUIDES

Compact Guide: Morocco is the ultimate quick-reference guide to this fascinating country. It tells you everything you need to know about Morocco's attractions, from historic ports to imperial cities, mountain resorts to desert oases and ancient bazaars to camel markets.

This is one of over 100 titles in Insight Guides' series of pocket-sized, easy-to-use guidebooks intended for the independent-minded traveller. Compact Guides are in essence travel encyclopedias in miniature, designed to be comprehensive yet portable, as well as up-to-date and authoritative.

D1507129

Star Attractions

An instant reference to some of Morocco's top attractions to help you set your priorities.

Mausolée de Mohammed V p19

Mosquée de Hassan II p22

Volubilis p31

Zaouïa de Moulay Idriss II p36

Tombeaux Saadian p39

Atlas Mountains p55

Erg Chebbi dunes p71

Kasbahs p72

Aït Benhaddou p78

Drâa Valley p79

Jemaa el-Fna p40

MOROCCO

Introduction

Places

Culture

Leisure

Practical Information

Morocco – A Taste of the Orient

Wherever you go in Morocco, you will be assailed by a unique variety of impressions that few other countries so close to Europe can match. From the mile-long beaches on the Atlantic and the Mediterranean to the green mountains of the Rif, from the remoter peaks of the High and Middle Atlas to the desert areas in the south, this is a land of huge contrasts.

In the ancient bazaars of the imperial cities of Meknès, Fès and Marrakech, the aroma of spices, bunches of peppermint, fresh bread and wood-shavings hangs in the air; strong colours dazzle the eyes, and the sound of the smithies' hammers resounds through the alleys. In the south, on the far side of the Atlas, ancient kasbahs with their battlements dot the date-palm oases bordering the Sahara, evidence of the wealth with which the settlers of these oases once derived from the caravan trade. The modern metropolises such as Rabat, the seat of government, or the economic centre Casablanca complete the picture.

Enticing spices

Seen from the west, Morocco is the Bab el-Maghreb, the gateway to the Maghreb. El-Maghreb simply means the west, or in rather more poetic terms, the place where the sun sets. From the east, thus for the inhabitants of the Near and Middle Maghreb, the Libyans, Tunisians and Algerians, Morocco is the far west, the western outpost of the Islamic cultural sphere. In Morocco, advanced forms of Islamic civilisation merged with ancient Berber traditions, and the magnificent buildings of the sultans were not purely Oriental but constructed in the Hispano-Moorish style. Morocco's unique cultural legacy is the result of numerous influences.

Berber welcome

5

Compared with its Islamic neighbours, Morocco is not a poor country. One indication of this is all the building that is going on, which is not limited to the major towns where progress and economic growth are the order of the day. Here, the traditional and the modern have always complemented one another admirably. Moroccans are proud of the 'golden mean' that governs their approach to life, and point to the conflicts in the neighbouring countries, where for years the Islamic fundamentalists have been the cause of violent conflict and economic isolation. Morocco is a country which is not opposed to progress while keeping its traditional values.

Position and landscape

Occupying the northwest corner of Africa, Morocco has 500km (300 miles) of Mediterranean coast while its west coast, stretching approximately 3,000km (1,860 miles) from Tangier to La Gouira,

is washed by the breakers of the Atlantic. As the state on the southern side of the Straits of Gibraltar, Morocco, borderd by Algeria in the east, guards this strategically important stretch of water 14–44km (9–27 miles) wide, together with Spain and British Gibraltar.

In an area of 458,730 sq km (117,116 sq miles), plus Western Sahara's 242,120 sq km (93,583 sq miles), there is a wide variety of landscapes: cultivated coastal plains and river valleys alternate with plateaux, which give way to high mountain ranges with dense mountain forests, followed by a gradual changeover to high steppe. In the far south this is bordered by date-palm oases, sand dunes and the stony desert (Hamada). Like a barrier, the Rif Mountains run along the Mediterranean coast. The highest point of this alpine chain is Jbel Tidiquin at 2,448m (8,031ft). The dominant Atlas Mountains divide Morocco into the fertile northwest and the desert-like, dry southeast. In the Middle Atlas the highest peak is Jbel Bou Naceur (3,340m/10,958ft). South of this the fold mountains of the High Atlas form a chain 700km (435 miles) long which includes the 4,165-m (13,670-ft) Toubkal, the highest mountain in Northern Africa. On the northern edge of the Sahara the final barrier is formed by the Anti-Atlas,which is 450 million years old and includes the 2,531-m (8,304-ft) Jbel Adrar-n-Aklim.

Climate and when to visit

The heart of Morocco, like southern Europe, belongs to the temperate climatic zone of the subtropics with dry summers and wet winters. The southern edge with the Western Sahara, on the other hand, marks the transition to a desert climate. The mountain ranges such as the Rif or the Middle and High Atlas and Anti-Atlas of course also affect the regional microclimate and are responsible for the considerable temperature variations in the interior.

Generally speaking, there is an even maritime climate along the coasts, and a continental climate with large temperature variations over the year in the rest of the country. Dark rain clouds frequently pile up in front of the ranges of the Middle and High Atlas, ensuring good agricultural soil for the farmers in the valleys, whereas on the other side of the peaks in the southern provinces rainfall is in short supply.

On the north and northwest slopes heavy showers can also occur outside the rainy season – from November to March – which cause devastating floods. Winter announces its arrival with heavy snowfalls in the high mountains. Ski resorts such as Oukaïmeden south of Marrakech are enjoying increasing popularity.

The best time to visit Morocco is in spring and autumn. In the interior of the country and on the southeastern high

The lush Ourika Valley south of Marrakech
Desert migrants

plateaux the thermometer climbs to an average 30°C (86°F) in the summer, while the cooler coastal areas at this time are perfect for swimming with temperatures of 22–25°C (72–77°F).

Summer in the High Atlas

Flora and fauna

7

In addition to the ubiquitous camels, cattle, horses, donkeys, mules, sheep and goats (all domesticated), Morocco has a rich and varied wildlife. There are animals typical of hotter climatic regions, for example the Barbary ape, a tailless monkey belonging to the macaques family, usually indigenous to Asia. There are also still predatory animals to be found such as the lynx, the jackal, the striped hyena, the red fox and the fennec (a desert fox) in the south. Mongooses and wild cats also live in Morocco, and very rarely in the Atlas you can spot the sure-footed but timid dorcas (mountain gazelles). The forests of the Atlas abound with wild boars as well as aoudad (wild sheep).

The bucolic Majorelle Gardens, Marrakech

Morocco is a popular breeding place for European migratory birds. Here you find numerous storks, finches, larks, swallows, thrushes, bee-eaters, guinea fowl, falcons, golden eagles, common ravens, desert ravens, pelicans, cormorants, herons, flamingos, seagulls and terns.

There are also reptiles: the gecko, the North African girdle-tailed lizard (a vegetarian), as well as the chameleon. The most common lizards are Berber skink (sandfish), and desert monitor lizards. The most common snakes are the common and puff adders, but you probably won't see any because they are too timid. Beware of scorpions during night time.

The sandfish or Berber skink

As far as vegetation is concerned, very little has remained of what were once vast wooded areas in the mountains and along the Mediterranean coast. In areas with more than 600mm (24 inches) annual rainfall the most common trees are holm and cork oaks, cedars, juniper, thu-

Dates from the oases

Desert dunes at Merzouga

jas (cypress family) and various conifers, while in the Anti-Atlas the argan (oil is extracted from the kernel of its fruit) predominates. In the southern coastal region large areas are covered with Moroccan ironwood and jujubes, a fruit tree. Across the mountains in the semi-desert areas, vegetation is sparse and, in the northeast, Spanish grass with its rushlike leaves is dominant. The most common plant in Morocco's oases north of the Sahara is the date. Reforestation with pine trees, poplar trees and eucalyptus trees has only been partly successful.

In order to protect endangered plants and animals, Morocco has created national parks and reserves. Of the five wetland areas in the country, four are on the list of the Ramsar Convention (*see page 59*). The gazelles and wild sheep are particularly in need of protection.

Population and religion

Broadly, Moroccans may be divided into urban and rural populations. The so-called Arab/Berber divide is now generally dismissed as a myth propagated during the French and Spanish protectorates. Today many Moroccans are of mixed ancestry, Berber and Arab.

The Berbers are the indigenous Moroccans. Their origins, however, are uncertain; theories include the possibility of European derivations, probably based on the not unusual occurrence of fair colouring and blue or green coloured eyes. The Berbers are of three main types (subdivided into countless tribes): the Riffians of the north; the Chleuhs from the Middle and High Atlas; and the Soussi, found in the southwest.

Around 40 percent of Moroccans still speak one of the three Berber dialects – Tamazight, Tachelait and Tarifit – as their mother tongue. In areas where the Berber population is in the majority, only the men are able to make

Village life

themselves understood in Arabic too. Berber remains incomprehensible to most Arabs.

When, from the 7th century onwards, waves of Islamic conquerors swept across the Maghreb to spread the divine revelations entrusted to the Prophet Mohammed, the Berbers voluntarily embraced Islam, becoming fanatical adherents (though they retained elements of pagan pantheism, still evident today in rural areas). Indeed it was the Berbers who led the Muslim invasion of Spain in the 8th century; impelled to spread the faith by the sword, they routed the Visigoths and initiated seven centuries of brilliant civilisation at a time when the rest of Europe was still in the Dark Ages. In secular matters, however, the Berbers always remained inplacable; their rebellious nature was most manifest in the mountainous hinterland and the south, where outside influences failed to get much of a foothold until the French and Spanish occupied the country.

In addition to the Arab/Berber population are the dark-skinned Moroccans (Haratines), who are descended from slaves and mostly live in the oases.

The once large and culturally important Jewish communities in the cities have today shrunk to a total population of 16,000. Many Jews emigrated to Morocco from Spain to escape the Inquisition, but at Independence in 1956, most of the Jews emigrated to Israel because they feared the Islamic religion would become stronger.

Morocco, however, stands out as a country where a wide variety of ethnic groups and tribes coexist without conflict. The total population is now 28 million with 60,000 foreigners, mainly French and Spanish. There is a strikingly large number of children: 40 percent of the population is under 15 years old, but the government hopes that the urgently needed further reduction in the population growth (from the present statistic of 4.2 children to two children per family) will take place as a result of the family planning now largely practised.

About town in El-Jadida

Children everywhere

The state religion is Islam. A few important brotherhoods are also represented, but most Moroccans are members of the Sunni faith. Religion penetrates all areas of daily life. It is not limited to the *Allahu akbar* of the *muezzin*, which resounds far and wide five times a day, but also determines marriage, divorce, inheritance, personal cleanliness, eating and drinking habits. Visitors during Ramadan, the fasting month of the Muslims, will find the faithful abstaining from eating, drinking and smoking from sunrise to sunset, and indulging in opulent feasts once the cannon has been fired to end the day's fast.

All these regulations are laid down in the Koran, the Hadith and the Sunna. The political head King Hassan II is also the *Amir almu'minin* – leader of the Islamic faithful in his country.

Customs

There is no doubt that Moroccan society is in the throes of radical change. One sign of the modernisation very diplomatically promoted by the king is the disappearance of the veil from the streets of the big cities. In Rabat, Fès or Casablanca it is only older women who do not yet feel able to discard it. The 'Islamic headscarf' is now very much in evidence instead. By contrast with the conventional headscarf, which as a fashionable, casually tied accessory leaves some of the hair free, this headscarf completely covers the hair. It is a different matter in the countryside and the remote mountain regions: in spite of the change that is noticeably in progress everywhere, here the conventional rules of behaviour are still a fixed part of daily life.

For ceremonies such as marriage, birth, circumcision or pilgrimages, even the women and men in the towns, who normally follow European-style fashions, don traditional dress. On official occasions in the palace or at the opening of a new parliamentary term, tradition is the order of the day.

The headscarf preserves modesty

Economy

It was not by chance that the signing of the world trade agreement GATT and the Middle East and North African economic summit took place in Morocco in 1994. It was a way of rewarding the country for its endeavours to achieve a more stable, export-orientated economy.

Measures such as the privatisation of state enterprises and a reform of the stock exchange in Casablanca have recently strengthened the economy and are attracting an increasing number of foreign investors to the country. Morocco is gradually leaning in the direction of the European market. Phosphate, citrus fruits, textiles, olive oil and tinned fish are the most important exports. Most goods are shipped from the modern harbour of Casablanca. Morocco is the largest exporter and the third largest producer of phosphates in the world. The main focus of economic development is on the promotion of agriculture through the building of further dams for irrigation systems, the development of export-orientated branches of industry and tourism. Fishing is also important.

Local catch

Government and politics

Many African states look with envy at the firmly established constitutional hereditary monarchy of Morocco, which since the early 1990s has become increasingly democratic. With its elected parliament, multi-party system, unions, a free and astonishingly varied press and its capitalistic economic order, Morocco is one of the most liberal of the Islamic countries, without sacrificing its Arabic-Islamic identity in the process.

The national flag

The king is head of state and commander of the armed forces. Legitimised by his direct descent from the Prophet Mohammed, he is however also 'Commander of the Islamic faithful' in his country and, according to Islamic belief, has the *baraka*, Allah's blessing, which renders him 'inviolable and sanctified'. Tremendous power is thus concentrated in the monarch with his double function as the highest secular and spiritual dignitary. In the 1980s, King Hassan II (who came to the throne in 1961) chose to underline his piety by having an enormous new mosque (inaugurated in 1993), costing five billion dirhams, built in Casablanca. Generally speaking, the project was supported by the people, who were each asked by house-visiting officials to contribute to the expense of building it – their present to their king for his 60th birthday.

Although the constitution underwent large-scale revision in 1992 and 1996, when the regions were strengthened by the creation of a two-chamber parliament, the king still appoints the prime minister and the incumbents of the highest civilian and military posts. Hassan II has earned respect in the West through his role in the Middle East peace process.

11

Administration

In the wake of the regional reform, there was an increase in the number of *wilayas*, the town prefectures with district prefectures under them. The other administrative units are provinces, divided into districts (*cercles*), community associations (*caïdate*) and communities. The *wilaya* is administered by a *wali*, the prefecture and province by a governor (both appointed by the king), the district by a *chef de cercle*, the *caïdate* by a *caïd* (both appointed by the Minister of the Interior) and the community by an elected chairman.

King Hassan II and the Palais Royal in Rabat

Historical Highlights

From 8000BC the first Berbers appear in the area. They leave rock drawings of the animals common at the time.

1200BC Phoenician seafarers found trade settlements, which are later taken over by Carthaginian merchants.

146BC After the fall of Carthage, the influence of Rome spreads west through North Africa.

24BC The Berber Juba II rules over the Roman province of Mauretania Tingitana from the capital Volubilis, near modern-day Meknès.

AD42 Mauretania becomes the Roman province of Mauretania Tingitana.

681 Muslim Arabs under the command of Oqba Ibn Nafi invade the country.

788 Moulay Idriss I, a descendant of Mohammed, is welcomed by Berber tribes in Volubilis and founds Morocco's first Arab dynasty.

807 Idris II founds Fès. Shortly after, Muslim refugees arrive from Andalusia in Spain and Kairouan, Tunisia.

1061–1147 Sanhaja Berbers from Western Sahara sweep northwards as far as Spain and establish the Almoravid dynasty. Founding of Marrakech.

1133–1248 Atlas Berbers from the Masmouda tribe, enemies of the Sanhadja, found the Almohad dynasty. At its peak, their empire stretches from Spain to Tripoli and represents the flowering of Moorish architecture.

1248–1465 The Merinid dynasty, founded by Zenata Berbers, a nomadic tribe from eastern Morocco. Portuguese and Spanish forces encroach on coastal cities.

1492 Fall of Muslim Spain. Muslims leaving Andalusia go to Morocco, in particular to Fès.

1554 Sherifs, descendants of the Prophet Mohammed, found the Saadian dynasty. Christians driven out of the country.

1664 Sherifs who settled in the Tafilalt Mountains in the 12th century found the present Alaouite dynasty.

1672–1727 Brutal but effective rule under the tyrannical Moulay Ismaïl in Meknès.

1860 The Spanish colonial towns of Ceuta and Melilla repel an attack by the Rif Berbers.

1873–94 Under Sultan Moulay Hassan the domestic political situation improves for a limited period. Under his successor Sultan Abdelaziz (1894–1908), Morocco is left bankrupt and open to European encroachment.

1912 The Treaty of Fès. Morocco is divided up between the colonial powers France (which gets the lion's share) and Spain. Tangier becomes international.

1920s Thami el-Glaoui connives with the French, pacifying rebellious tribes in exchange for power and privileges (*see opposite*).

1927 The Alaouite Mohammed Ben Youssef ascends the throne as Mohammed V. In 1953 he is sent into exile.

1930s/40s An independence movement centring on the Istiqlal Party emerges in Fès. Growing unrest is met with repression.

1956 Dissolution of the protectorate under pressure from the Moroccan people. Morocco declares its independence. Political leader is Mohammed V, back from exile since 1955, who changes the title of Sultan to King.

1961 After the death of Mohammed V, his eldest son, Hassan II, succeeds to the throne.

1963–67 King Hassan survives five different plots against him, the most serious of which are led by the army.

1975 The Green March. The King leads 350,000 unarmed men and women to claim the Western Sahara for Morocco. Phosphate mining commences, as does the development of the infrastructure of the Saharan provinces.

1976 Backed by Algeria, the liberation organisation known as the Polisario disputes Morocco's claims on Western Sahara. Morocco's relations with Algeria deteriorate.

1988 Relations between Morocco and Algeria are restored. A referendum is promised to determine the fate of Western Sahara. The old North African dream of pan-Maghreb unity is revived.

1989 Founding of the Union du Maghreb Arabe (UMA – Union of the Arabic Maghreb).

1992 The long-promised referendum in the Western Sahara is postponed by UN observers because of accusations of vote-rigging.

1993 The Hassan Mosque opens in Casablanca.

1996 In a referendum in September, 99 percent of the voters are in favour of a changeover to a two-chamber parliament.

1997 The Parliamentary elections result in a narrow majority for the Socialist Union of Popular Forces (USAP), and Abderrahmane Youssoufi is nominated prime minister in February 1998 after more than 40 years in opposition.

1998 The referendum on the future of Western Sahara finally scheduled for December.

The Protectorate

'30 March 1912 to 18 November 1955: 43 years, 7 months and 18 days – the shortest protectorate in colonial history,' wrote the editor of a Moroccan newspaper with a hint of pride on the anniversary of the return of Sultan Mohammed V from exile.

The Berber and Saharan tribes in particular, with their fierce desire for freedom, repeatedly rebelled against the central powers in the course of Moroccan history. Although the religious authority of the sultan was at no time seriously challenged, at the beginning of the century there was a deep rift running through the population of the country, making it almost ungovernable.

For centuries Morocco had been split into two parts, one of which consisted of large sections of territory kept under strict control, while the other comprised the areas settled by the less loyal Berber tribes, who vehemently resisted any form of subjugation and taxation.

This situation was exploited by the colonial powers France and Spain when they set up their protectorate. Thami el-Glaoui (1872–1955), the powerful leader of the Glaoua clan, allied himself with the French during the protectorate, and in recognition of his services was made Pacha of Marrakech by the gouverneur général. This opportunist ruled over a large part of southern Morocco. He won the trust of the French landowners and industrialists and even attempted to topple the sultan. After Mohammed V's triumphant return from exile, the Berber prince went down on his knees to the monarch and begged for forgiveness. He died a short time later. His legacy and that of his clan live on in several mighty places and kasbahs in Marrakech and south of the Atlas Mountains.

Despite such allies, it was not until 1934 that the colonial powers succeeded in bringing about a temporary peace in the country, after a period of violent uprisings in the Rif and Tafilalt Mountains. They were spearheaded by another Berber chief, Ben Abd-el-Krim (1880–1963), otherwise known as the 'Wolf of the Rif Mountains'. Abd-el-Krim was born into a respectable Berber family and gained a traditional education at the famous Karaouiyne University in Fès. After a career in the Spanish colonial government, in 1921 he became leader of the Resistance movement in the Rif, and embarked on a series of military campaigns. After the decisive battle near Annoual on 17 July, he proclaimed the autonomous Republic of the Rif.

Together with his tightly organised army of 75,000 partisans, Ben Abd-el-Krim gained further succcesses but was finally brought to surrender in 1926 by the 250,000-strong Franco-Spanish army under Marshall Pétain. He was then exiled to the island of Réunion in the Indian Ocean; granted amnesty in 1947, he went to Egypt where he formed the North African Liberation Committee. Ben Abd-el-Krim is now honoured as a national hero.

The irony is that it was only the colonial power, during a brief and eventful protectorate, that succeeded in developing the modern, comprehensive Western-orientated infrastructure that led the country into the modern age. What was even more important, however, was that the mere fact of its presence had the unintentional result of uniting all the various groups in successful resistance against the French and Spanish occupying powers.

Mausolée de Mohammed V

Route 1

Rabat *See map on page 18*

Centre of power

Andalusian Gardens detail

The main square, Place Moulay Hassan, is bright and cheerful with its splendid display of seasonal flowers beneath old rubber trees. King Hassan is known to be fond of lavish floral decoration, so there is obviously going to be no shortage of plants in his capital (pop. 1.7 million with Salé). However, this does little to hide the social gap between the south of the city and the north.

Inland, far away from the noise and air pollution, is the villa quarter of Souissi, where high walls conceal subtropical gardens containing swimming pools. The Ville Nouvelle (*see page 81*) is the busy centre: its main boulevard, Mohammed V, has a number of public buildings in a 1930s style, but one junction beyond are the run-down apartments of the middle classes. Finally, the walled medina in the original kasbah quarter facing away from the Atlantic above the estuary of the Bou Regreg river is primarily home to the poor.

History

The cliffs where the Oudaïa Kasbah stands today were originally the site of a *ribat* (fortified monastery) built in the 10th century by Berbers who had converted to Islam. In 1150 the Almohad Abd el-Moumen built a kasbah with a mosque on the site of the ruined *ribat*.

His grandson Abou Youssef Yaacoub el-Mansour (1184-99) moved the royal capital of his large realm, Rabat el-Fath, (the Rabat of Victory), further south. The 6km (3.7 miles) of walls, fortified by bastions and five

Preceding pages: Aït-Benhaddou

monumental portals, had only just been completed when he died. The square minaret of the unfinished grand mosque, the Tour Hassan, is still one of the city's landmarks. The half-finished Rabat fell into ruin when the sultans who succeeded him transferred the capital back to Marrakech.

Tired shoppers

In 1609 it was resettled by Jews and Muslims returning from Al-Andalus. When the kasbah became too crowded, they founded the present-day medina and protected it on the south side with the Andalusian wall. In the following period it was primarily these settlers who openly opposed the central power of the Saadians. They declared the 'Republic of Bou Regreg' and financed their state by organised piracy, with which they terrorised the seas until the beginning of the 19th century.

The attractive core of the Ville Nouvelle was built during the French protectorate. The colonial power developed the Almohad capital as its administrative centre. Since then, the municipality has expanded far beyond the Almohad walls with soulless suburbs spreading southwest. The seat of government and capital of the country is completely overshadowed by the economic metropolis of Casablanca, but it does have a very famous university, the Université du Mohammed V.

City Tour

All the sights of the inner city can be reached on foot. Independent travellers will find their way easily round Rabat without having to use a guide.

Begin a tour of the city at the complex surrounding the symbol of Rabat, the **Tour Hassan** , which is entered through a narrow gateway, flanked by two guards of honour on horseback. Abou Youssef Yaacoub el-Mansour, founder of Rabat and the most important ruler of the Almohad dynasty, commissioned the building of a mosque in honour of victories in Spain at the end of the 12th century. It was to be the second largest in the Islamic world, but when Yaacoub el-Mansour died four years after building began, the work was stopped and the mosque fell into ruin, with the earthquake of 1755 accelerating the process.

Tour Hassan and detail

You enter a large, open area dominated by the square, reddish-brown minaret, the Tour Hassan, on the northern side. Extending from the tower is a forest of columns, all that has remained of the planned 19 naves of the prayer hall of the Almohad mosque. The 44-m (144-ft) minaret was one of the three pillars of the great Almohad realm, along with the minaret of the Koutoubia mosque in Marrakech and the Giralda in Seville. Its stone relief decoration is an example of the elegant simplicity of Almohad art in the 12th century.

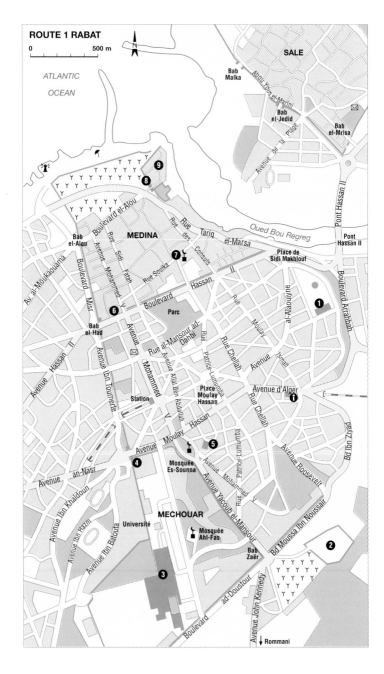

Opposite is the ★ **Mausolée de Mohammed V**, built between 1961 and 1971 (daily 9am–6pm, entrance free). The guard of honour patrols the marble mausoleum as you walk round it. In the interior there is a gallery looking down onto the sarcophagi of King Mohammed V and his son Moulay Abdallah.

Guarding the mausoleum

A rather longer and very pleasant walk takes you down the Avenue Mohammed V, with its subtropical vegetation and important ministries in elegant colonial style, to the 2,300-year-old ruins of ★ **Chellah ❷** (daily 9am–6pm). The complex lies outside the Almohad wall on the Bab Zaër and is also surrounded by a high wall.

The Carthaginians are known to have founded a trade settlement here in the 3rd century BC. Later the Romans built the river port of Sala, and from the 13th century the Merinids used the deserted area as a necropolis. It was only during the reigns of Abou Saïd (1310–31) and Abou el-Hassan (1331–51) that the earth walls were built round the cemetery, the entrance to which was a massive portal with two turns in it, projecting bastions and stone reliefs in Kufic script. The tomb of the Sultan Abou el-Hassan is one of the most interesting, with its artistic inscriptions. Next to it is the grave of his wife with the pretty name of Shams ed-Douna (The Light of Dawn). With a jungle garden, and the reddish minaret of the Merinid mosque rising out of the middle of it, its domed marabouts and the storks and egrets which build their nests on wall projections and the trees, Chellah has its own, rather poetic atmosphere.

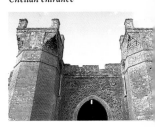

Chellah entrance

Go back through the Bab Zaër to the ★ **Palais Royal ❸**, which was built in 1864 and enlarged by Mohammed V and Hassan II. The buildings, visible from outside, are roofed with the typical green-glazed tiles; and palace guards patrol in front of the ceremonial Moorish portals. There is a great deal of nervous activity when sirens sound in the distance, and minutes later a convoy of cars, escorted by heavy motor bikes, speeds through the main gate. Wasn't that the King, sitting behind reflecting windows in one of the cars?

The **Bab er-Rouah ❹** the 'Gate of the Winds' was the most important entrance in the Almohad wall. The monumental structure is lightened with beautiful Koran suras, arabesques and the typical decorative shells. Today it stands at a noisy road junction with traffic roaring past in the direction of Casablanca and Agdal. The domed rooms of the gate complex are frequently used for exhibitions.

Not far from the Mosquée Es-Sounna in Avenue Mohammed V, is the ★ **Musée Archéologique ❺** (23

Palais Royal

Rue el-Brihi; 9–11.30am, 2.30–5.30pm, closed Tuesday). This national museum has the most important archaeological findings from prehistoric, Phoenician, Carthaginian and Roman sites in Morocco. Displayed in a glass case is a fragment of the jaw of a *homo erectus*, dated around 400,000BC. In a separate building are the wonderful bronze sculptures from Roman Volubilis (*see page 31*).

After a little window-shopping under the arcades along the right-hand side of the busy Avenue Mohammed V, a coffee stop on the shady terrace of the Balima Hotel will be very welcome. Crowds of people, the din of traffic, shoe-blacks and lines of taxis are the dominant features of the **Marché Central** ❻ (closed Friday and Sunday afternoons) at the entrance to the ★ **Medina**. On Thursdays and Saturdays, when the locals stack the fresh produce they have bought by the crate-load into their cars for their large families, it is particularly busy. The rectangular, roofed market area dates from the 1920s.

An Oriental atmosphere predominates along the Rue Souika, the most important shopping street in the medina, where the poorer sections of the population provide one another with the necessities of life. The light is dim in the thatched-roof section, the Rue es-Sebat, with its many shoe shops. To the right is the simple minaret of the **Grande Mosquée** ❼. It was built in 1882, replacing a previous building on this site. The top of the minaret was only added in 1939.

In the Rue des Consuls are rows of shops selling a great variety of carpets. With the words '*pour le plaisir des yeux*' ('just looking'), the dealers try to entice passers-by into their shops. At the end of the carpet souk stands the Great Gate, the ★ **Bab el-Kebir** ❽, the main entrance to the Oudaïa Kasbah. At the end of the 12th century Yaacoub el-Mansour built this bastion on the highest point of the kasbah. The most magnificent gateway to be erected during Almohad rule, it is splendidly decorated with *guilloches* and Kufic inscription bands.

Oudaïa Kasbah

The ★ **Oudaïa Kasbah** ❾ stands on the site of the 10th-century Berber *ribat* mentioned above. The **Mosquée de la Kasbah** dates from the 18th century, and replaced a building from the time of Abd el-Moumen (around 1150). Moulay Ismaïl recruited mercenaries from the Oudaïa tribe and stationed them in this kasbah. A medieval charm pervades the narrow streets of this living area with its whitewashed, flat-roofed houses. And the Andalusian **Jardins des Oudaïa** (daily 8.30am–6pm, entrance free), although only added in 1915 by the French, blends harmoniously into the kasbah complex. The small palace, which Moulay Ismaïl

Tiles from the Jardins des Oudaïa

The Musée des Oudaïa

built on the north side of the garden, is today used by the **Musée des Oudaïa**, with arts and crafts, jewellery, traditional costumes and old musical instruments.

Finally the nostalgic **Café Maure** with blue stools and shady, tiled wall seats in the open air is an ideal place to take a break. From here there is a view across the steep banks of the Bou Regreg river to the walled old town of Salé.

Excursion to Salé

You can reach the historic heart of the town of **Salé** (580,000 inhabitants) and its remarkable buildings by *taxi collectif* (collective taxi) or bus across the Pont Hassan II, or by rowing boat across the river.

In the Middle Ages, the inhabitants of Salé conducted brisk trade with European merchants, and the Moorish palaces still standing in the medina testify to their prosperity. From 1609, Salé was settled by Muslim and Jewish refugees from Al-Andalus who were feared as notorious pirates, and retaliations by the affected European fleets were inevitable.

Like all towns with populations of Andalusian refugees, Salé too was a centre of sophisticated craftwork. However, with the rise of its rival Rabat, the town went into economic decline from 1912.

Pottery in Salé

Among the most interesting cultural sites in Salé is the **Medersa Abou el-Hassan**, the former Koran school which dates from 1341 (daily 9am–noon, 3pm–6pm). Its beautifully decorated inner courtyard has an elegant gallery supported by 16 columns. There is a splendid view from the roof terrace. Next door is the oldest sacred building in Salé, the **Grande Mosquée**, founded by the Almohads.

In the former bastion Borj Sidi Ben Achir, dating from the 18th century, is the **Musée de la Ceramique**.

Grande Mosquée d'Hassan II

Route 2

Casablanca

Hectic business metropolis

As the seat of big business and service suppliers, Casablanca (pop. 2.9 million) is primarily of interest to business travellers, trade fair visitors and adventurous boat owners. The nostalgically minded who have travelled far to find traces of a certain world-famous film will search in vain. Humphrey Bogart will be encountered only as a poster on the wall of a bar or as a look-alike on a bar stool. A new attraction, however, is the Grande Mosquée d'Hassan II which has added a spiritual focus to this hectic business metropolis. The new symbol of the kingdom, which gleams from afar, acts as a magnet for both pilgrims and sightseers from all over the world.

Casablanca's modern streets otherwise reflect the tolerance practised by the Moroccans. Women with daringly slit skirts walk side-by-side with their modestly covered Islamic sisters, for whom the wearing of the Islamic headscarf is not a matter for debate.

Houses near the port

History

The elegant quarter of Anfa was originally the location of a Berber settlement of the same name, founded in the 8th century. It was not only the merchant ships that set sail from here for Europe, but also the much faster little pirate ships. While the former were engaged in the lucrative grain trade, the latter were just as successful with their plundering exploits along the Portuguese coast. Piracy came to its inevitable end in 1468 with the destruction of the pirates' den by the Portuguese fleet. In 1575 the conquerors constructed a new harbour and called it Casa Branca (White House). In 1755 the invaders were driven out of this unsafe corner of their realm, but by 1782 Spanish merchants were already trying their luck here. Now the trading post was called Casablanca, in Arabic Dar el-Beïda. An increasing number of Europeans came to settle here until the mid-19th century, but were forced to leave again when violent attacks were directed against them.

Casablanca's greatest period of prosperity began in 1912, when the first French governor Lyautey set about transforming it into an international port and the economic centre of the protectorate of Morocco. Until only very recently the thriving city was still attracting numerous rural migrants, who mainly settled on the edge of the city in the spreading 'canister towns' or *bidonvilles*.

Local artisan

23

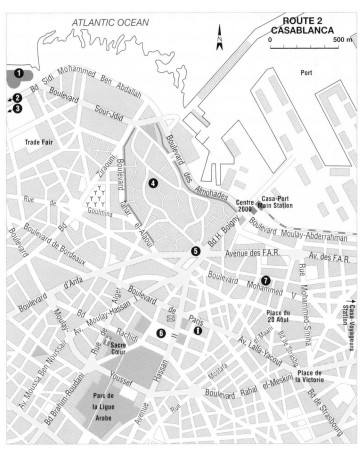

Thanks to a model resettlement programme, most of these slums have disappeared.

Today, 59 percent of Morocco's manufacturing industry is located in the Casablanca area. The chemical, textile, foodstuffs and metal industries predominate. Greater Casablanca is the most populous part of the country, with eight district prefectures, and is the seat of the modern Université d'Hassan II.

City Tour

'And Allah's throne was on the water...' Impossible to miss, the ★★ **Grande Mosquée d'Hassan II** ❶ (Bd Sidi Mohammed Ben Abdallah; guided tours daily except Fridays and on Islamic holidays) is the dominant feature of the skyline when you approach the city from the sea. With this modern religious building – and not only Muslim but also Jewish and Christian dignitaries were invited to the consecration ceremony in August 1993 – the King established himself in the eyes of the world as a champion of a tolerant Islam.

Grande Mosquée d'Hassan II

From the 200-m (656-ft) green-and-white minaret a 30-km (19-mile) long laser beam points the way east across the night sky towards Mecca. This monumental building, conceived for 105,000 faithful, was designed by the French architect Michel Pinseau, and 90 engineers and 30,000 Moroccan workers and craftsmen were involved in its construction. The earthquake-proof building complex includes a medersa (Koran school), a national museum, several traditional *hammams* (baths) and an underground garage. The adjoining theological library is the largest in the Islamic world. It is linked by computer with all the large libraries in the world. Even the prayer room is high-tech: the electronically controlled sliding roof opens in only three minutes.

More than 12 million people contributed, not always on a voluntary basis, to the collections made to help finance the 'Eighth wonder of the world'. It cost the equivalent of around £300 million and involved the destruction of a whole quarter of the city, whose residents had to be rehoused. This is the only active mosque in Morocco open to non-Muslims, who must pay a fairly hefty entrance fee. Though the area open to them is fairly small, it does offer the chance to see the work of some of Morocco's finest contemporary craftsmen.

Taking a dip at Aïn-Diab

Take a taxi along the Nouvelle Corniche to **Aïn-Diab** ❷, the coastal strip to the west of the city. Here the French built several sea-water swimming pools in the rocks, which are a popular destination of the city dwellers during the summer months. Around 3km (1.9 miles) further on, picturesquely located on a rocky head-

land, is the **Marabout de Sidi Abderrahman ❸**. At flood tide the grave of the holy man is cut off from the mainland. His *moussem*, a big festival in August lasting for several days, attracts large numbers of people from the surrounding area.

Place Mohammed V

The holiday playground of Aïn-Diab is worlds apart from the busy **Medina ❹**. The tiny area which is all that remains of the old town is hemmed in between the Ville Nouvelle and the fishing port. There is no comparison with the medinas of such famous cities as Fès and Marrakech, and here there is a startling contrast between the old centre and the office skyscrapers of the adjoining New Town which overshadow it.

Adorned with shooting fountains and graced by four imposing neo-Mauresque buildings, the magnificent **Place des Nations Unies ❺** is both a busy traffic junction and the transition point between the traditional medina and the hectic new town. A domed pedestrian subway and a Hyatt Regency hotel give the junction its international air.

Casablanca's boulevard, the Avenue Hassan II, runs south, leading to the finest square in the city, the **Place Mohammed V ❻**. Stylish administration buildings from the time of the protectorate, built during the 1920s and including the official seat of the *wali* with a 50-m (164-ft) clock tower and the Palais de Justice, surround a green oasis with seats under tall palm trees. On the other side of the road the monumental fountain (erected in 1965) is a magnet for pigeons and children – when it is operating.

Want a snack?

The Boulevard Mohammed V, Casablanca's old main shopping street, is undeniably Gallic in character, lined with a fascinating variety of decorative facades in the architectural style of the 1930s. The lively **Marché Central ❼** is also from this period.

Place el-Hedim

Route 3

Meknès

Power and grandeur

All the projects of Moulay Ismaïl, the second sultan from the house of the Alaouites, were conceived on a grand scale. Over a period of 55 years, the power-obsessed autocrat turned his capital Meknès (pop. 530,000) into the largest fortified town in North Africa.

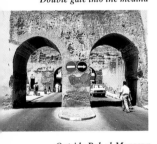

Double gate into the medina

The imposing remains of Ismaïl's storehouses and defensive walls with their gigantic gates still dominate the city. The mausoleum of the Sherifs alone is one of the most magnificent in the country. The chronicles record 30,000 slaves and at least 500 ladies of the harem. Moulay Ismaïl went down in history as the most powerful of all the Alaouite sultans, who ruled his country with an iron hand and guaranteed peace and order.

The city walls are the most impressive feature of all, almost 20km (12 miles) long and dominated by the huge Bab el-Mansour. The slaves laboured under the most demeaning conditions on this most ambitious building project of their master, whose successors used the stone largely as a quarry.

Outside Bab el-Mansour

Set in olive groves close by are two significant historical sites: the Roman ruins of Volubilis and the Muslim place of pilgrimage Moulay-Idriss with the mausoleum of Idriss I, founder of the first Arabic-Islamic state on the territory of present-day Morocco.

History

In the 10th century, Meknassa Berbers were attracted by the abundant supply of water, fertile agricultural soil and olive trees on the banks of the Oued (river) Boufekrane. They called their scattered village Meknassa ez-Zitoun.

Under the Almoravides, a fortified settlement was built on the site of the present medina, which subsequently acquired mosques, medersas and wall fountains from the Almohads and Merinids. Viziers of the Merinid rulers, whose court was in neighbouring Fès, had second residences in Meknassa.

The city's greatest period of prosperity, however, came when the Alaouite Moulay Ismaïl (1672–1727) succeeded to the throne. This self-willed ruler raised the status of Meknès above that of the two royal seats of Fès and Marrakech to make it his capital; in the unprecendented building boom that ensued, every one of the state buildings reached giant proportions, in accordance with the excessive nature of the tyrant. To decorate his colossal works of architecture he plundered the Roman city of Volubilis *(see page 31)* and the Saadian Palais d'el-Badia in Marrakech *(see page 40)*. After his death the city declined as quickly as it was built, but the remaining ruins still give a good idea of its splendour and size.

In 1912 the French founded a Ville Nouvelle *(see page 81)* on the opposite side of the river and established

Market encounter

27

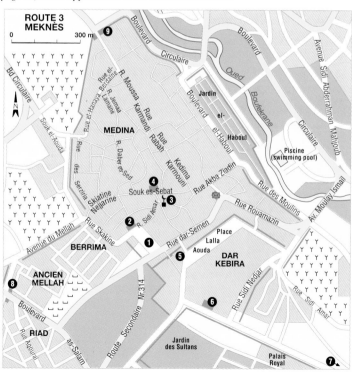

one of the most important agricultural and wine-growing areas in Morocco on the Meknès-Saïss plateau. Meknès is today an important crafts centre and seat of the university of Moulay Ismaïl.

City Tour

For a relaxing tour of town

The medina begins at the **Place el-Hédim** ❶ in the melée of taxis, shoe-blacks perched on tiny stools, travelling hawkers and bizarrely attired water-sellers. However, before you plunge into the labyrinth, on the other side of the pointed-arched gateway next to a pretty Moorish wall fountain (1914) is the **Musée Dar Jamaï** ❷ (daily 9am–noon, 3pm–6pm; closed Tuesday). A long winding hall with a brightly painted carved ceiling ends in an idyllic inner garden. This was the house of the grand vizier Mohammed Ben Larbi Jamaï, dignitary at the court of Moulay Hassan (1873–1894). Jamaï fell out of favour during the uprisings under Sultan Abdelaziz (1894–1908) and died in prison. In the Moorish rooms are examples of regional arts and crafts, such as priceless wooden carvings, jewellery, ceramics and Berber carpets. On the upper floor the private and reception rooms of the vizier can be seen. These interiors are an interesting example of the high quality of Moroccan home décor around the turn of the century.

28

From the peace and quiet of these elegant surroundings you are plunged into the hustle and bustle of the adjoining souk. To the right of the fountain a gate opens into the new **Kissaria de bijoux**, a paradise if you are looking for Oriental jewellery.

Jewellery display

At the heart of the souk is the **Grande Mosquée** ❸. The prayer hall is still lit by a chased chandelier inscribed with the name of the Almohad Sultan Mohammed en-Nasir (1199–1213). Moulay Ismaïl had the mosque renovated in 1695 and added the valuable pulpit (*minbar*).

Once, in the midst of the noisy Souk es-Sebat, the double doors with bronze reliefs opened into a haven of peace and quiet. Look up to see above the alley a carved dome, the unmistakeable mark of the ★★ **Medersa Bou Inania** ❹ (daily 9am–noon, 3pm–6pm). Now no longer used as a Koran school, the medersa was built during the rule of Abou Inans (1351–58), who was also responsible for the famous college in Fès. Of the 50 student rooms, several have no windows, while others have tiny slits facing the narrow alley. Only privileged pupils had rooms facing the quieter inner courtyard. The refined decoration of the courtyard comes as a surprise: tile mosaics, plaster stuccowork, friezes of inscriptions with Koran suras and cedarwood carving. At the centre of the courtyard is a marble basin in the shape of a shell for the ritual ablutions before prayer. The impressive Moorish wall decorations are continued in the prayer hall and reach perfection in the frame around the five-sided prayer niche.

After Moulay Ismaïl had concealed his city behind a 40-km (25-mile) long protective wall, he modelled his architectural complexes on similar structures in far-away France built for his contemporary Louis XIV. Finally, he not only maintained flourishing trade relations with the king, he even went so far as to ask for the hand of the princess, which was, however, refused him by the French court.

Nevertheless, Ismaïl went ahead with the building of an imperial city, the *Ville Impériale*, south of the medina: 30 palaces alone were built, separated by gardens with pavilions and ponds, barracks, stables and an enormous storehouse.

The giant gate ★ **Bab el-Mansour** ❺ has survived the centuries as the most imposing reminder of these times. The sultan's life's work, it was completed by his son and successor Moulay Abdallah in 1732, and is of majestic proportions. The triumphal arch is decorated with white marble columns and composite capitals from the Roman town of Volubilis (*see page 31*). Since 1995 it has been used as an art gallery.

The mausoleum of the eccentric sultan was naturally substantially enlarged by his successors, the dynasty that is still ruling today, and was restored by Mohammed V. Together with the mausoleums of Idriss I in Moulay-Idriss, Idriss II in Fès and Mohammed V in Rabat, the ★★ **Mausolée de Moulay Ismaïl** ❻ (daily 9am–noon, 3pm–6pm, Friday closed until 3pm; entrance free) is one of the most important such shrines in Morocco. Beneath

Mausolée de Moulay Ismaïl, door detail

Bab el-Mansour

Tilework on the mausoleum

the canopy of the gate facade, the inscription translate as 'Mausoleum of the great monarch Moulay Ismaïl, son of Ali Chérif, proclaimed sultan 1032 (= 1672), died in Meknassa ez-Zitoun Saturday 28 Redjeb 1139 (= 1727), may Allah save his soul.'

Non-Muslims may enter the mausoleum but must take off their shoes in the lobby and from here can look into the lavishly decorated room holding the tomb. Above the sarcophagus, surrounded by a grille, is a 12-sided carved dome.

Moulay Ismaïl not only maintained a substantial royal household, an international harem with 500 women of all races and a countless hoard of children, but also the famous 150,000 black troops and an army of slaves, one of whose tasks was to look after the 12,000 horses on his stud farms.

The double building of **Heri and Dar el-Ma** ❼ gives some idea of the gigantic proportions of Ismaïl's city. The storehouse, 180 by 69m (591 by 226ft) and a good 12m (39ft) high, divided into 23 aisles by clay pillar arcades, was used for grain, while under the high vaults of the 77 by 69m (253 by 226ft) Dar el-Ma were cisterns 40m (130ft) deep, from which water was drawn by water wheels rotated by horses or camels.

From the terrace of Dar el-Ma there is a panoramic view of the 400 by 100m (1,312 by 328ft) Aguedal irrigation tank, the present royal palace and the ruins of the old Dar el-Makhzen, with the medina of Meknès beyond.

Finally, mention should be made of the two other decorative gates in the wall. The **Bab el-Khemis** ❽, the west gate, dates from 1687 and originally opened into the garden quarter where the ruler's viziers lived; at a later date the Thursday market was held here. The **Bab el-Berdaïne** ❾, built some years later in 1709, with its ornamental bastions, diamond-shaped glazed-tile decorations and arabesques, resembles the older west gate.

Excursion to Moulay-Idriss and Volubilis

Numerous buses and *taxis collectifs* run from the Bab el-Mansour to the shrine at ★★ **Moulay-Idriss**, 27km (17 miles) from Meknès. The whole year round this small town, clustered picturesquely round two outcrops of rock, is full of pilgrims. On the **Sahat Massir al-Khadra** (Square of the Green March), with its terrace café, the Muslim pilgrims buy decorative candles for the shrine and sweets for their families. A wooden barrier marks the beginning of the *horm* (holy area), which non-Muslims are not allowed to enter.

The national shrine is the resting place of the historic figure Moulay Idriss I (788–793). When he founded the

Pilgrim to Moulay-Idriss

first Islamic state on Moroccan soil, with what later became Fès as the centre of power, this Arabian ruler ushered in a new epoch in the extreme northwest of the African continent. The sanctuary was given its present form by two Alaouite rulers: Moulay Ismaïl in the early 18th century and in the 19th century the extravagant Sultan Moulay Abderrahman. From the **Mosquée Side Abdallah el-Hajja** there is a view of the town with the mausoleum complex under green-tiled roofs.

Below the Zerhoun Mountains, 5km (3 miles) northwest of Moulay-Idriss, lies an important ancient site, the ruins of the Roman town of ★★ **Volubilis** (daily 8.30am–5 or 6pm). As the capital of the African province of Mauretania Tingitana, it flourished both economically and culturally in the period from AD42–285. At the beginning of its history, it had an unusually long period of peace, which made a defensive wall unnecessary.

The ruins, excavated and partly reconstructed by French archaeologists, including the Capitol, forum, triumphal arch, basilica and baths, demonstrate how prosperous the inhabitants once were; the 50 olive presses that were found show that olive oil was a prime source of their wealth. In the atrium and peristyle houses of the patricians were magnificent bronze sculptures which are today housed in the Musée Archéologique in Rabat (*see pages 19–20*). With their fresh colours, the mosaic floors look as if they were only recently laid. The naturalistic animal figures and an imaginative ensemble of sea creatures in the House of Orpheus are particularly worth seeing.

It was only when the attacks by the Berbers became more frequent that a wall with 10 gates was built round Volubilis. Finally the city went into decline and the Romans retreated to Tingis, present-day Tangier.

Views of Volubilis

31

The triumphal arch

Bab Bou Jeloud, gateway to Old Fès

In the depths of the souk

Route 4

Fès

The heart of Arabo-Islamic culture

In Fès el-Bali it is if nothing had changed since the Islamic Middle Ages, if you ignore the bicycles and television aerials. To be pushed along the narrow alleys by the crowds, get stuck in a traffic jam consisting of donkeys, smell the penetrating aroma from the tanneries, spice dealers and hot food stalls and be dazed by the insistent noise from the craftsmen's workshops is already an experience in itself; this is further enriched by treasures of Moorish architecture so important they have been added to UNESCO's World Cultural Heritage list. The old city centre, complete and enclosed within its walls, appears timeless. It is dominated by the minarets of the mosques with their roofs of green-glazed tiles; green was the colour adopted by the Prophet's descendants. Today a focus of history and culture, Fès (pop. 770,000) is still one of the most important places in the Maghreb.

History

Fès is the cradle of the Moroccan monarchy. Its first representative was the political refugee Moulay Idriss I, a great-grandson of the Prophet's daughter Fatima. After an unsuccessful uprising he fled in 786 from his home, Medina, to Volubilis. The Berber tribes living there listened to his sermons about Islam and in 788 appointed him their *imam* (holy leader). In this function, Idriss I accelerated considerably the spread of Islam and the Arab influence in the Maghreb. He assembled his followers by the River Fès in a camp by the name of Madinat Fas. In 793, two months after his death, his son was born, who at the age of 11 was appointed imam. Later, Moulay Idriss II (804–828) transformed the Berber camp of his father into an Oriental-Arabian capital.

Educated Arabs from Kairouan in Tunisia, experienced craftsmen from the caliphate of Córdoba, as well as the business activities of numerous Jews contributed to the city's rapid rise to prosperity. With the building of the Karouiyne Mosque in the year 859, a tradition of Koran interpretation was begun which is still greatly respected in the Islamic world.

Fès reached its cultural high-point in the 13th and 14th centuries as the residential town of the Merinid sultans. Until 1912, the oldest of the four sultan towns, it was the political, economic and cultural centre of the country. When the French transferred their centre of power to Rabat and Casablanca, Fès remained the focus of the country's spiritual life.

City Tour

Although like all Moroccan cities Fès consists of a walled Arabic medina and a new town – Ville Nouvelle – laid out by the colonialists, the old town is in turn divided into Fès el-Bali (Old Fès) founded in 800 by the Idrissids, and the later Fès el-Jdid, which goes back to the Merinids of the 13th century.

View over Old Fès

The attractive, rather southern-European Ville Nouvelle is bisected by the wide, palm-lined Avenue Hassan

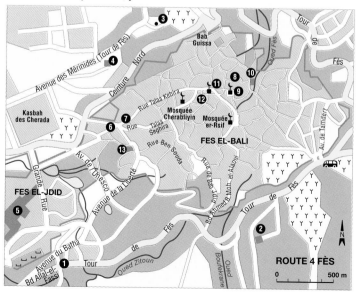

ROUTE 4 FÈS

0   500 m

Close encounter

II with interesting old public buildings roofed with green tiles. In the Place Mohammed V, with its decorative group of trees, the three corner cafés – La Renaissance, Le Cristal and La Koutoubia – are pleasant places to pass the time.

Before you get hopelessly lost in the confusion of alleys, the 16-km (10-mile) ★★ **Tour de Fès** ❶ is recommended, with three places from which to view the whole city. The circuit of the two medinas begins on the Place Mohammed V. Follow the Boulevard Allal el-Fassi and the turning up to the **Borj Sud** ❷, a fortress built in the 16th century by the Saadian Ahmed el-Mansour. The jumble of houses spreading up the hill above the river valley is Fès el-Bali. The horizon is dominated by the 902-m (2,959-ft) Jbel Zalagh. A *son et lumière* show has been held here every year since 1994 with the fort making an impressive backdrop.

A second bird's-eye view of the three city districts can be obtained from the hill with the few remaining ruins of the **Tombeaux Mérinides (Merinid tombs)** ❸. In the mausoleums are the remains of the last Merinid sultans. There is a no less attractive view from **Borj Nord** ❹, the counterpart of Borj Sud. The exhibition rooms here have a comprehensive collection of historic weapons.

The starting point for a tour of the medina of ★★ **Fès el-Jdid** is the **Palais Royal** ❺. This huge palace complex (not open to the public) was begun by the Merinids and has been continuously enlarged ever since. Behind the gilt bronze portals of the monumental gate, built only in 1969–71, are extensive palaces, gardens, parade squares, a Merinid medersa and a mosque.

★★★ **Fès el-Bali** is entered through the **Bab Bou Jeloud** ❻. This tripled-arched gate, dating from only 1913, was built in the traditional Moorish style. The outer side is decorated with panels in a diamond-shaped pattern of blue-glazed tiles, while the side facing the medina has green faïence arabesques.

Picturesquely framed in the archway are two minarets, the smaller one belonging to the Mosquée Sidi-Lazzaz, the larger one to the ★★ **Medersa Bou Inania** ❼, one of the country's few buildings in religious use that can be entered by non-Muslims (daily 9am–noon, 2.30–5 or 6pm; closed during Friday prayers until 3pm). With the medersa that bears his name, Abou Inan created the largest and most splendid Islamic college in Fès. Built between 1351–58, it is concealed behind a high brick wall on the Talaa Kebira. Only the small windows with their wrought-iron grilles suggest

Bab Bou Jeloud

that this was a centre of study. In the courtyard is a splendid display of Merinid craftwork. Tiles made of onyx and white Carrara marble, mosaics of glazed tiles, Koran suras carved in stucco and stalactite friezes of cedarwood all testify to the aesthetic leanings of the ruler who built it. The most lavish decoration is to be found in the *mihrab* (niche) in the prayer hall.

The silent **Bou Inania water-clock** also belongs to the medersa. This 14th-century clock, constructed at the behest of Abou Inan to ring out the hours of prayer, has been silent for five centuries. Before restoration work was commissioned by UNESCO some years ago, 13 little bronze hammers struck the same number of bronze bowls resting on the carved cedarwood supports. But it has not yet been possible to get the clock going again: its ingenious mechanism continues to defy the world's best horologists.

There is a bewildering contrast between the meditative stillness of the medersa and the noisy **Talaa Kebira** (Big Hill), which goes down into the labyrinth of Fès el-Bali. Hammering and banging resounds from the many little shops and workshops that are completely open to the street. Loaded donkeys steer a path through the crowds accompanied by the drovers' cries of '*Balak balak*', warning people out of the way.

Spoilt for choice

In the winding streets of the Souk Attarine is another splendid example of Merinid art: the former ★★ **Attarine Medersa ⓼**, built by Sultan Abou Said in 1322, has an inner courtyard of great elegance. As the medersa is no longer in use you can enter the prayer hall, and it is also possible to gain access onto the roof for views of the green roofs and the blue and white tiled courtyard of the Mosquée Karaouiyne.

The green roofs of the Mosquée Karaouiyne

Mosque detail

Around the ★★ **Mosquée Karaouiyne ❾** the crowds grow denser. Today, Lalla Fatima al-Fihrya, the pious woman from Kairouan in Tunisia, would not be able to recognise the little prayer hall that she built for her compatriots in 859: with an area of 16,000sq m (170,000 sq ft), it is the second largest mosque in Morocco and one of the most splendid in the world; but even more significantly it is the most important Islamic university of the western hemisphere. Its present appearance was the work of the Almohads and Merinids. In the 16th century the Saadians added two beautiful fountain pavilions in Andalusian style to the richly decorated courtyard. The library, installed in the 13th century, has a unique collection of old illuminated Koran manuscripts which are gazed on with awe by every Muslim visitor. The 16-aisled prayer hall has space for 20,000 worshippers and is supported by 270 pillars made of marble and porphry. Non-Muslims can only gain a faint impression of all this splendour by peering through one of the 14 bronze doors decorated with relief patterns.

If you don't want to be put off by the smell of ★★ **Les Tanneries ❿** (closed Friday), buy a bunch of mint and hold it to your nose as you walk through. The methods used here have not changed for centuries. The fresh animal hides are steeped in urine to make them supple, although in spite of opinions to the contrary, chemicals are now used at least for the removal of the hair from the pelts, before they are immersed in the tubs. To get the best views of the eggbox network of pits where the skins are soaked and dyed, you need to climb up to the terraces where they are laid out to dry.

Zaouïa de Moulay Idriss II has a wealth of inticate detail

The narrow alleys in front of the ★★ **Zaouïa de Moulay Idriss II ⓫**, the mausoleum of the founder of

Fès, are full of pilgrims. Gifts are sold in the tiny shops around it and there are stalls selling almond and sesame biscuits, white nougat, dates and nuts. Pilgrims choose from the large selection of ornamental candles on display as offerings. The Moorish shrine with the tomb of Moulay Idriss II acquired its present form between the 18th and 19th centuries. The faithful place their donations in the bronze-lined opening in the south wall, next to a wall fountain with coloured stucco ornamentation. As part of the ritual they kiss the wall which conceals the sarcophagus of the patron of Fès. Visitors can look into this place of worship through the magnificent doors, which are kept open.

Zaouïa de Moulay Idriss II

The ★ **Place Nejjarine** ⓬ has been charmingly restored and has a former *fondouk* (inn) with a richly decorated monumental gate, a pretty canopy and a delicate, Moorish-style wall fountain. The aroma of cedarwood wafts from the neighbouring Souk Nejjarine, where the carpenters who gave the square its name still pursue their trade in the restored workshops.

Those with a particular interest in folk art should allow plenty of time for a visit to the ★ **Musée Da Batha** ⓭ (Place de l'Istiqlal; daily 9am–noon, 2.30pm–5.30pm; closed Tuesday). The Alaouite vizier palace, dating from the end of the 19th century, has the most comprehensive collection of arts and crafts in Morocco. The extensive palace complex in Moorish style is in itself an experience. The magnificently carved and painted double doors of the exhibition rooms open onto a garden courtyard laid with mosaics. Illustrated Korans, ceramics, carved furniture, woven articles, embroidery, carpets, wrought iron and, in particular, fragments of Moorish wall ornamentation, are enthralling.

As the centre of Islamic learning, Fès has also founded a 'Festival of world religious music', which is now an annual event taking place in May/June with performances of Islamic, Jewish and Christian music in old Moorish palaces. Further information is available from the Association Fès-Saïss, tel. 635400.

Excursion to Moulay Yacoub

Since 1993 the small spa village of **Moulay Yacoub**, 20km (12 miles) north of Fès, has been twinned with the French spa Aix-les-Bains. Buses to the village leave from the Bab Bou Jeloud (*see page 34*).

The focal point of the original spa is the **Marabout of Moulay Yacoub**, above the miracle-working hot sulphur spring. In 1989, below the original village built on terraces, a new spa was opened to treat rheumatism and ear, nose and throat disorders. Here belief in miracles and orthodox medicine go hand in hand.

Place Jemaa el-Fna

Route 5

Marrakech *See map on page 41*

Jardins de la Majorelle, detail

Gateway to the south

In the summer, a paralysing heat broods over the city of Marrakech, in the winter the snowy peaks of the High Atlas glitter from afar. The massive, clay-coloured defensive wall of the medina contrasts with the southern-looking vegetation of the Ville Nouvelle (*see page 81*). It is not without reason that the most important city in central Morocco (pop. 745,000) is called the 'Red Pearl'. The earthy red of the ramparts and the houses of the spreading double town is typical of the architecture of the pre-Sahara. Taxis rattle along the avenues of the *Ville Nouvelle*, heavily laden donkeys trot through the crowded, sunlit alleys of the medina. While the old palaces hide their splendour behind forbidding walls, craftsmen proudly show off their skills in tiny workshops. Globetrotters succumb to the charm of Marrakech, and snobs justifiably swear by its uniqueness. Whether you choose to stay in a Moorish luxury hotel or in a colonial garden villa, or are obliged to make do with one of the basic hotels, after you have escaped the Place Jemaa el-Fna teeming with tourists, Marrakech is something straight out of an Oriental fairytale.

History

Shortly after they came to power, in the year 1062 the Almoravids established a camp here at this strategically important location just to the north of the Atlas Mountains. This rapidly became a Berber settlement and by 1126–27 the capital of the Almoravid realm was surrounded by a defensive wall. From 1147, the city prospered under the Almohads and it was in this period that the famous Koutoubia mosque was built. In the 13th century the ruling Merinids then transferred the capital to Fès. Their successors the Saadians, however, moved it back to Marrakech again in the 16th century, and with the flourishing caravan trade with black Africa and the export of raw sugar brought it to a new peak of prosperity. At this time Moulay Ahmed el-Mansour ad-Dahbi built the legendary Palais d'el-Badia.

From 1912, the Haouz Plain was settled by numerous French colonists, and the finest colonial city in the Maghreb was created outside the walled medina at a height of 453m (1,486 ft). Trade, agriculture and tourism still guarantee a balanced economic structure. The town is also the seat of the university of Cadi Ayad.

City Tour

For 800 years the 77-m (252-ft) minaret of the ★ **Mosquée Koutoubia** (mosque of the booksellers) **❶**, built by the Almohads, has been the symbol of the city and the whole of the Haouz plain. The 3-km (2-mile) long Avenue Mohammed V, lined with Seville orange trees, would be unthinkable without this ochre-coloured tower and its characteristic arched windows, elegant tracery and diamond reliefs. Behind the closed portals of the mosque are 17 aisles, their horseshoe-shaped arches supported by capitals decorated with plant motifs. Next to the tower is a *koubba* for Lalla Zohra Bint el-Kouch, daughter of a prince from black Africa who lived in the 17th century and is revered as a saint.

Anyone interested in Moorish art will, of course, be keen to visit the ★★ **Tombeaux Saadian** (Tombs) **❷** (daily 8.30am–noon, 2.30–6pm). Moulay Ahmed el-Mansour ad-Dahbi (called 'the Golden') built the double mausoleum in the second half of the 16th century and 62 members of the Saadian dynasty are buried here. The simple graves of the courtiers are laid out in the shade of fan palms, mandarin and thorn apple trees. The tombs were only rediscovered in 1917, having been bricked up by the Alaouite Moulay Ismaïl in the late 17th century.

Tombeaux Saadian and detail

The Hall of the Twelve Columns in the main tomb is rated the most perfect architectural work of this epoch. On the walls of the mausoleum, polychrome tile mosaics, stuccowork inscription friezes and intricate arabesques are masterfully blended to form a filigree decor of great beauty. Beneath the carved dome made of gilt cedarwood, supported by 12 white monolithic pillars made of Carrara marble, are the three magnificent sarcophagi of Sultan Ahmed el-Mansour, his son and successor and his grandson. In the stalactite niche of the

The ruins of the Palais d'el-Badia

smaller mausoleum is Lalla Messaouda, mother of the Sultan, with numerous ladies of the court buried close by. The high infant mortality rate of the times is documented by the many small graves.

The remains of his **Palais d'el-Badia** ❸ bear witness to the wealth accumulated by Moulay Ahmed el-Mansour through the gold and slave trade. Arab chroniclers write of 360 rooms, each one expensively designed with Carrara marble, onyx, faïence mosaics, stuccowork and carved ceilings covered in gold leaf. However, this splendid creation of the most powerful of the Saadians was demolished by the equally powerful Alaouite Moulay Ismaïl in a fit of jealousy a century later. The ruins, which since 1960 have provided the setting for a folklore festival usually held every June, are nevertheless most impressive.

The lifestyle of a Maghreb grand vizier at the end of the 19th century is illustrated by the ★ **Palais Bahia** ❹ (9am–noon, 3pm–6pm, closed when the King is in Marrakech). Covering an area of 6 hectares (15 acres), it has 150 rooms with double doors opening onto gardens, fragrant with jasmine and citrus fruits, and marble-tiled inner courtyards gleaming in the sun. The luxury of an Oriental court is reflected in all the reception and private rooms. Bahia, the 'radiantly beautiful' woman who gave her name to the palace, bore the grand vizier Ba Ahmed a son, as the first of his four legitimate wives.

The **Dar Si Saïd** ❺ (daily 9am–noon, 3pm–6pm; closed Tuesday) is worth seeing not only for its exquisite collection of regional arts and crafts. The Moorish palace, which was built in 1895 at the same time as the Palais Bahia, was the home of the grand vizier Ba Ahmed's brother, Si Saïd, a chamberlain and vizier of Hassan I. The richly carved and colourfully painted ceilings and double doors of these rooms are fine examples of the sophisticated wood-carving of this period. In glass cases along the walls are valuable pendants, caftans, copper articles, and real and ornamental weapons. On the second floor are original Berber carpets.

Jemaa el-Fna scenes

On the central square of ★★ **Jemaa el-Fna** (the meeting place of the dead) ❻, the heads of those who had been executed used to be mounted on long spears and put on display. Today, in the late afternoon, it is the travelling performers who attract the attention of both tourists and local people. Although the look of the place has been changed radically since the wooden stalls were torn down in the 1980s, the show goes on. In 1994 the Jemaa el-Fna had to be given another 'face-lift' and now has neat lines of drinks stalls. In the evening the mobile kitchens move in, each providing an astonishing array of snacks cooked on the spot and eaten at the adjoining tables. Evening entertainment is provided by snake charmers, story-tellers, acrobats and whirling Gnaoua dancers with their huge iron castanets.

'In the souks it is spicy, cool and colourful,' wrote Elias Canetti in his book *The Voices of Marrakech*, after visiting the city in 1954. The ★★★ **souks** ❼ of the medina of Marrakech are the most extensive in Morocco. Divided according to craft, the workshops and shops of the potters, wool-dyers, metal-workers and wood-turners are open to the critical or curious eyes of the passersby. In the dyers' quarter, garishly coloured, dripping bundles of wool hang from the house walls, the Kissaria is hung with shimmering Oriental caftan materials and glittering ladies' *babouches* (slippers) cover the walls of the tiny shops, and in the copper bazaar beautifully shaped vessels wink in the sunlight. Between the shops,

In the dyers' quarter

41

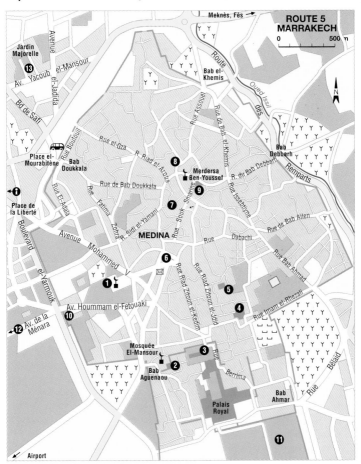

ROUTE 5
MARRAKECH

0   500 m

arched doorways under carved canopies lead into a *hammam*, an old *fondouk* or a mosque. Every quarter has its wall fountain, where girls fetch water. Under a canopy, a Kufic inscription on the monumental fountain **Echrob ou Chouf** ❽ exhorts passers-by to 'drink and admire'.

The splendidly decorated ★★ **Medersa Ben Youssef** ❾ (daily 9am–noon, 3pm–6pm) was founded by the Merinid Abou el-Hassan in the 14th century, and developed by the Saadians as the largest Koran school in the Maghreb. Through double doors with bronze reliefs the visitor enters the white-tiled courtyard made of Carrera marble with a pool at the centre. An octagonal carved dome arches over the prayer hall, dimly lit by small arched windows with pierced filigree stuccowork. Inside, many of the rooms have been given over to temporary art exhibitions.

Medersa Ben Youssef

Between 6–9m (20–30ft) high, and fortified by approximately 200 bastions, the city wall of packed clay is a massive construction. A trip round it (*Tour des Remparts*) is something not just for the romantically inclined, but is also of interest as an illustration of medieval defence techniques. Combine the ride in a horse-drawn cab with visits to the 10 differently constructed gate buildings. The 13-km (8-mile) tour starts at the **Bab el-Jdid** ❿. The Bab Aguenaou is especially worth a stop, with its rich stone relief decoration, as are the Bab Ahmar, a vaulted passage 17m (56ft) deep, the Bab Debbarh (the bastion looks down on the tubs of the tanners) and the 21m (69ft) deep Bab el-Khemis.

A detour to the olive grove of **Aguedal** ⓫ (daily 8.30am–6pm) is also to be recommended. It was laid out in the 12th century by the Almohads and walled by Hassan I. From the water tank, in the right weather conditions, the silhouette of the nearby Atlas Mountains can be seen.

The trip by horse-drawn cab just before sunset along the 2.5-km (1½-mile) stretch from the Bab el-Jdid to **Ménara** ⓬ (8.30am–6pm) is not just something for honeymooners to do. As the sun goes down, the olive grove, the Almohad water tank and the pretty Moorish pavilion are bathed in a magical golden light.

Jardins de la Majorelle

In the north, a further detour for a walk along the winding paths of the **Jardins de la Majorelle** ⓭ (Avenue Moulay Yaacoub el-Mansour; daily 8am–noon, 2pm–6pm) is the ultimate exotic experience. The combination of a fascination with Oriental gardens and fantasies about the Garden of Eden resulted in this special garden on the edge of the new town. In the park surrounding his villa, the painter Jacques Majorelle (1886–1962) planted the botanical souvenirs collected on his many journeys through Africa from the Atlas to the Ivory Coast. With the many different greens of the plants set in azure tubs or in beds framed in the same colour, together with pools and waterfalls reflecting the sun, Majorelle created a uniquely beautiful work of art. Delicate bamboo plants and islands of cacti contrast with the bright colours of the abundant flowers, reflecting the compositional skills of an aesthete, and each season presents a different picture. Water dominates the park: in azure-blue canals, fountains and lily ponds.

The property was restored some time ago by the French fashion designer Yves Saint-Laurent.

Excursion to the Atlas
Oukaïmeden – Ourika

When seen on a clear winter's day from the ramparts of Marrakech, the snow-capped Atlas Mountains seem almost close enough to reach out and touch. And in reality their northern flanks are little more than an hour's drive away.

The Atlas from Marrakech

The name **Oukaïmeden** (72km/45 miles) is synonymous with snow and skiing. The plateau, at a height of 2,650m (8,694ft) on the Jbel Oukaïmeden (3,273m/ 10,738ft), is provided with hotels and lifts and attracts many winter sports fans. Mountaineers make the descent to **Asni** (1,150m/3,773ft), while the less ambitious use their cars to explore the landscape and the earth-brick villages clinging to the hillsides.

43

Back down in **Arhbalou** (1,025m/3,363ft), follow the Vallée d'Ourika to **Setti-Fatma**, 24km (15 miles), at a height of 1,500m (4,921ft). As the starting point of trekking tours, the mountain village has a number of inns, and its rural restaurants also attract many visitors to this high valley.

Rural Vallée d'Ourika

Route 6

Tangier

Where seas and continents meet

The port of Tangier

'I feel at the moment like a dreamer gazing at things which he fears will vanish before his eyes,' wrote the French painter Eugène Delacroix during his stay in Tangier in 1832. The special atmosphere of this harbour town (pop. 526,000) is derived from the mixture of Arabic architecture and European and Arabic-Berber life-styles, together with a powerful shot of Spanish influence. The Straits of Gibraltar connect not only Europe and Africa, but also the Mediterranean and the Atlantic Ocean. Lingering over the bay of Tangier however is that hint of disrepute common to all ports, permeated by the melancholy of past glory. It is not advisable to walk about at night in the harbour or station area, or in the medina.

History

On his great voyage of discovery in the direction of the Gulf of Guinea, the Carthaginian seafarer Hanno anchored off Tangier, then called Tingis, in 5BC. In

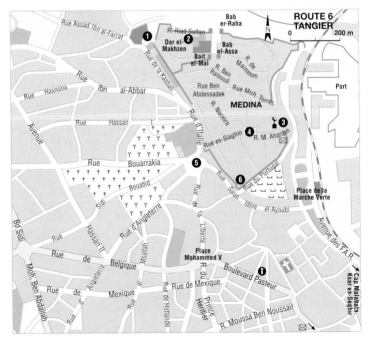

ancient times the whole province was the granary of North Africa. With the advance of the Muslim Arabs a new era began. The city fell successively to the Almoravids, the Almohads and the Merinids, and in 1471 was settled by the Portuguese. Through the marriage of Charles II to Catherine of Braganza, the city came under English domination in 1661, but the Alaouite Moulay Ismaïl forced the invaders to retreat in 1684.

In the late 19th and early 20th centuries, the strategically desirable port was an object of dispute amongst the European colonial powers and the German Empire also had economic interests in Morocco. When Tangier was declared an international zone in 1923, a fever of trade activity was unleashed and the new town expanded rapidly. When this special status ended in 1956, the attractiveness of the city began to wane. Only smugglers and drug dealers valued its proximity to the Spanish exclave of Ceuta. Today Tangier is pinning its hopes on a thriving tourist trade and industry. A technical college was founded and since 1994 further ambitious projects have been launched with the aim of restoring Tangier's former economic status.

Washing day

City Tour

Next to the relatively small medina is the new town, built parallel to the wide sandy beach. To the west is the district of Montagne, a green villa suburb where the palaces of the Moroccan and Saudi-Arabian royalty are also located.

In the northwestern corner of the old city wall, the **Bab el-Kasbah** ❶ opens onto the **Kasbah** ❷, the highest part of the ★ **medina**. Inside, the narrow Rue Riad Sultan runs along the northern part of the wall. The best panoramic view is from the terrace restaurant, Le Détroit. There is also a fascinating view of the Straits from the Bab er-Raha in the north wall.

Assortment of nuts

On the Place de la Kasbah, a horseshoe-shaped Moorish gate framed in brightly coloured glazed tiles leads into the two museums of the ★ **Dar el-Makhzen** (9am–noon and 3pm–6pm; closed Tuesday). In the former sultan's palace, which Moulay Ismaïl built in the 17th century, there are arts and crafts on the ground floor, and on the upper floor a collection of antiquities with copies of the important Hellenistic bronze sculptures from Volubilis (*see page 31*), the originals of which are in the Musée Archéologique in Rabat (*see pages 19–20*). In the entrance hall of the museum is the Bait el-Mal treasury. For centuries the cedarwood chests under the star-studded dome were used as strongboxes.

The Bab el-Assa, where floggings once took place, leads out of the Kasbah. Follow the busy alleys of the

45

souks down into the centre of the medina to the **Grande Mosquée ❸**, which Moulay Ismaïl built on the original site of a Roman temple.

The heart of the medina is the Spanish-looking **Socco Chico ❹**. In the 1920s, the area was a notorious red-light district, but today it has returned to normality. The Rue es-Siaghin, one of the most important shopping streets in the medina, opens into the **Place du 9 Avril 1947 ❺**. The busy junction is dominated by the minaret of the Mosquée Sidi-Bouabid with its coloured tiles.

The traditional good diplomatic relationships between Morocco and the USA are documented in the **Museum of the American Legation ❻** (8, Zankat America; 9am–12.30pm, 3pm–6.30pm; closed Tuesday). The exhibits in the 19th-century Legation building include the correspondence between George Washington and Sultan Moulay Abdallah.

Excursions

Cap Malabata – Ksar es-Seghir

The coast road runs more or less parallel to the long sandy beach. It passes several hotels and, outside the town, small beaches. From the east side of Cap Malabata (11km/7 miles) there is a view over the **Straits of Gibraltar**. Captains of ships from all over the world use a lighthouse as their marker when negotiating this narrow part of the much-travelled Straits, which are only 30km (19 miles) wide at this point. Day trippers and tourists watch the traffic on the water from the restaurant terrace while sipping their *thé à la menthe* (mint tea).

During the holiday season, the beach of **Ksar es-Seghir** (33km/20 miles east of Tangier) is very crowded. Unfortunately the ruins of the Portuguese fortress are misused as a latrine in the summer. A trip here by taxi is nevertheless worthwhile for the splendid views.

Cap Spartel – Grottes d'Hercule – Cotta

On the rugged rocky coast of **Cap Spartel** (14km/9 miles west of Tangier), the Mediterranean meets the Atlantic, making swimming a dangerous venture. Sunsets from the cape are often spectacular, and can be watched from the terrace of the fish restaurant Mirage (daily noon to midnight).

The **Grottes d'Hercule**, 4km (2½ miles) further south, were rock chambers inhabited in prehistoric times. Half a mile further on, close to the sea, are the sparse ruins of the Roman trading centre of **Cotta**, dating from the 2nd and 3rd centuries. So far, the foundation walls of a settlement, the vats used for pickling fish, a bath house and the remains of a temple have been excavated.

Guardian of the Straits

Cap Spartel

Route 7

On the trail of the Portuguese

**Agadir – Essaouira – Safi – El-Jadida – Casablanca
(540km/336 miles)** *See map on page 48*

The forts along the Atlantic coast from Agadir northwards to Casablanca are a reminder of the days when this seafaring nation was a force to be reckoned with. Rocky coasts are interspersed with endless wide sandy beaches, which are dotted with brightly coloured tourist tents in the summer. The scenery then changes to narrow coastal terraces, chequered with vegetable plots and salt gardens. And according to the season, there are undulating green or golden cornfields, or round, open-air threshing floors with donkeys plodding round them.

The gnarled argan trees special to this area predominate as far north as Safi. Amidst the thick branches goats demonstrate their tree-climbing skills willing to risk their necks for the luscious green fruit; the long-necked dromedaries have easier access.

During the bathing season families equipped with *khaïmas* (tents) stream to the cool Atlantic. Foreigners combine beach-life with visits to the white harbour towns. If you stay overnight in Essaouira, Safi and El-Jadida the car journey will take you four days.

Agadir (pop.185,000) was reconstructed in uninspiring concrete after the devastating earthquake of 1960, and has no special atmosphere, let alone a centre. By way of compensation there are 8km (5 miles) of splendid sandy beach, good sports, restaurant and entertainment facilities, a wide variety of hotels and the best tourist service in the country.

High season in Agadir

Agadir: a reconstructed town

Agadir, in short, has something for everyone. If you want to see something more of Morocco, go on at least one of the numerous excursions that are offered. In Agadir itself, the fishing and trade port can be visited and the weekend market is very popular. The hill on which the kasbah stood before the earthquake has a panoramic view of the city and bay.

The first stage of this route runs close to the coast. North of Agadir, golden sandy beaches invite you to stop for a swim. Not until **Tamri**, 56km (35 miles), where Morocco's best bananas grow, does the road veer away from the tempting sea to pass through gently rolling hills where argan trees grow densely in the reddish soil. Shortly after Tamanar, a side road curves down to **Cap Tafelney**. Here at the foot of the cliffs is a shallow sandy beach with fishermen's houses, barques and fountains. The road then climbs for 7km (4.3 miles) in the direction of Jbel Amsittene (905m /2,969ft) where there are wild pigs in the forest and a good view of the surrounding countryside.

The dunes just outside ★★**Essaouira** (pop. 56,000) are protected from the wind by acacias and junipers. It is not without reason that the women in this exposed town continue to wear their traditional *haïk*, the white or beige wool scarf that is draped in a complicated fashion to cover them completely. Though it had been developed as a trading port by the Arabs, the town as you see it today, with its rather unusual-looking medina and souks, was built entirely by Sultan Sidi Mohammed in the 1760s to replace Agadir as Marrakech's chief port. Formerly known as Mogador, a corruption of a Berber word for 'safe anchorage', it is perched on a rocky peninsula surrounded by fortifications, legacy of a brief Portuguese occupation in the 16th century. The unique architecture of the old town, with its straight roads and numerous arched passages, was the work of the French engineer Théodore Cornut.

The Porte de la Marine opens out onto the busy fishing port. At midday, the aroma of freshly grilled fish served at numerous stands pervades the air. Immediately behind the Porte de la Marine is the **Skala du Port,** with its threatening battery of Spanish cannons from

ROUTE 7

0   50 km

Casablanca

Rabat

Dar-Bouâzza

Aïn-ej-Jmel

Bir-Jdid

Tnine-des-Chtouka

Azemmour

El-Jadida

Moulay-Abdallah

Port de Jorf-Lasfar

Oued Oum er Rbia

Boulâouane

Sidi-Moussa

Sidi-Smaïl

Sidi-Bennour

Oualidia

Khemis-des-Zemamra

Cap Beddouza

Youssoufia

Safi

Bouguèdra

Sebt-des-Gzoula

Tnine-Rhiate

Oued Tensift

Talmest

Chichaoua

Sidi-Moktar

Marrakech

Ounara

Imi-n-Tanoute

Essaouira

Smimou

Jbel Amsittene 905

Cap Tafelney

Tamanar

Tamri

Taghazoute

Oued Sous

Oulad-Teïma

Agadir

Aït-Melloul

Inezgane

the year 1743. From up here there is a view of the town, the harbour, the bay and the offshore rocky islands, which are now a bird sanctuary but in the 7th century were used by Phoenician sailors on their trading forays down the west coast of Africa. Traditional crafts of the region, including inlaid cabinetwork, are exhibited by the **Musée des Arts et Traditions Populaires Sidi Mohammed Ben Abdallah** in the Rue Laalouj.

Top gun at Essaouira

In recent years Essaouira has made a name for itself internationally with its painters. Works by the most famous naive painters of the town can be seen in the **Galerie d'Art Frederic Damgaard** (Avenue Oqba Ibn Nafiaa, medina).

At **Ounara**, 197km (122 miles), the dense *thuja* woods give way to eucalyptus trees, followed by rolling hills. The industrial town of **Safi** (pop. 262,000), 299km (186 miles), is announced by high chimneys and the permeating smell of fish. Because of the chemical industry and the phosphate harbour, the coastal waters north and south of Safi are not suitable for bathing. The wall enclosing the medina with its bastions and the ruins of the Dar el-Bahr (Castle of the Sea) are reminders of the days when the town was under Portuguese rule, though the town reached the height of its prosperity under the Saadian sultans. Today, the fortifications are used during the summer months for a wide variety of cultural events.

49

Safi is proud of a pottery tradition that goes back centuries. Above the Bab Chaabah, in the ★ **Quartier de la Ceramique**, smoke rises from the kilns – some of them still wood-fired – of the largest ceramic centre in Morocco. The **Musée National de la Ceramique**, in the former governor's palace dating from the 18th century, documents the wide variety of these famous ceramics.

Pots drying in the sun
Pottery kilns in Safi

The **Marabout de Sidi-Bouzid**, 303km (188 miles), dominates the landscape on top of the cliffs north of Safi. The nearby Refuge de Sidi-Bouzid is an inviting restaurant to stop for lunch with a view of the harbour from its terrace. On Cap Beddouza is the second oldest lighthouse in Morocco, dating from 1915. Beneath it miles of sandy beach stretch northwards, and along the road are rows of greenhouses, used for growing tomatoes.

For gourmets **Oualidia**, 365km (227 miles), is synonymous with oysters, which can be tried in two restaurants (*see page 89*). Many wealthy Moroccans, including the King, have beautiful holiday homes in Oualidia. **Moulay Abdallah Amghar**, is the scene of one of the largest *moussems* (*see page 85*), held in the month of August in honour of the holy man of the same name whose mausoleum dominates the village. The festival is attended by the falconers of the province, who demonstrate the skills of their trained hunting falcons.

Along the sandy beach of Sidi-Bouzid, identified by its domed marabout tomb on the cliffs, is a further concentration of holiday homes owned by rich Moroccans.

El-Jadida ramparts…

★ **El-Jadida** (pop. 120,000), 441km (277 miles), is the capital of the province of the same name. In 1917 a *citerne portugaise* (Portuguese cistern) was discovered and excavated in the walled medina that was built in 1815 in place of the destroyed Portuguese city. It is the town's main attraction. In the 16th century, the underground columned hall with its late-Gothic, groined vault served as a munitions depot and later as a cistern. A beam of sunlight entering through the opening in the roof magically illuminates the room and the vaulting is reflected in water several inches deep covering the floor.

…and carpets

Azemmour (pop. 32,000), 457km (284 miles), picturesquely rises above the left bank of the Oum er-Rbia. In 1486 Portuguese merchants were entrenched in the kasbah. They were expelled in 1541, leaving their cannons behind, which are now historical relics decorating the park and the bastions. The **Bab Mellah** has steps leading up to the battlements. From here there is a view of the medina, the kasbah and the former *mellah*. The old town has splendid houses which would never be suspected within these walls. It was only when it became too crowded here that the new town was built.

The last stretch of the route leads through agricultural areas, past numerous greenhouses growing tomatoes and melons, and through corn, barley and wheatfields, or fields of stubble in the summer. Side roads lead down to various beaches along the way, and a hazy patch on the horizon indicates that **Casablanca**, 540km (336 miles), is not far away (*see page 22*).

Route 8

In the realm of the 'blue men'

Agadir – Tiznit – Guelmim (199km/127 miles) *See map on page 52*

Guelmim – one of the largest camel markets in Africa

51

On the far side of the Oued Massa the nearby desert announces its approach. This marks the start of the realm of the 'blue men', whose blue and white robes billow decoratively (and photogenically) in the wind. Until the 1960s, the Saharan tribes were still leading a nomadic life with their camel caravans in an area reaching into black Africa. Modern means of transport however forced most of them to settle in one place and pursue a wide variety of occupations. Only a few of them continued as nomadic livestock breeders. These tribesmen still live in their tents and sell their sheep and dromedaries in the souks. The camel markets of the 'blue men' remain one of the most exciting experiences of a holiday in Morocco. Guelmim continues to profit from its long outdated reputation as being one of the largest camel markets in Africa, but although the Saturday souk is today a perfectly ordinary livestock market, it is still well worth a visit. In order that the tourists who have come here specially do not go away disappointed, fake 'blue men' are only too ready to act as photographic models or play the part of caravan leaders.

An overnight stay in Guelmim is recommended, preferably from Friday to Saturday, in order to be in the souk towards 8am. Don't forget to reserve a room. Two days should be allowed for this route.

On the road to **Inezgane**, 11km (7 miles) south of Agadir, are several hotels for those anxious to avoid

Looking the part

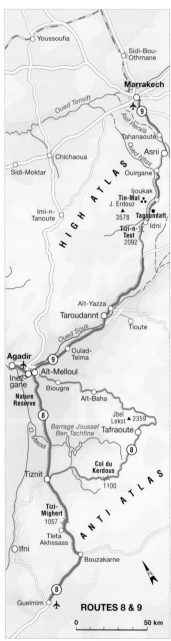

Agadir, or who have been unable to find a room there. Otherwise this crowded commuter town, a bus junction, has a dreary suburban atmosphere. Just outside the busy trading centre of **Aït-Melloul**, 13km (8 miles), the road crosses the Oued Sous, a river which plays a vital part in the area's agriculture.

In 1991, the national park of **Sous-Massa** (33,800 hectares/83,520 acres) was created in the coastal area between the estuaries of the Oued Sous and the Oued Massa. The bird that it is particularly designed to protect is the bald ibis, which is threatened with extinction and only breeds in Morocco. In 1994, addaxes (large antelopes) imported from Germany, Denmark and France, gazelles from Western Sahara and ostriches from Chad were introduced here. The 460 hectares (11,370 acres) of reedy wetlands at the estuary of the Massa are the home of many marsh and water birds, including pink flamingos.

On the other side of the Oued Massa begins the dry province of Tiznit. In the distance is the reddish silhouette of the provincial capital of the same name, which was built on an equally red desert plateau. The important trading centre of **Tiznit** (pop. 43,000), 91km (57 miles), originally consisted of 10 kasbahs. It was not until 1882 that it was surrounded by a 4km (2½ miles) wall, built in the reign of Hassan I. When in the course of time the town became overcrowded within its protective walls, a new pre-Saharan settlement was developed outside them, which with its pale ochre buildings has its own particular charm.

The main gate, known as the Gate of the Three Windows (marked by the Moroccan Star) leads into the medina and the **Méchouar**. Once the parade ground of the French soldiers garrisoned in the town, it is now the lively main square bustling with donkey carts, cars with horns blaring, buses and people battling their way across it. Around the sides are hotels and cafés under Moorish arcades, and small shops concealed behind blue doors. Steep steps lead up to the cheap hotels on the top floor of some of the houses, simple quarters for travelling salesmen.

The dominant feature of the medina is the minaret of the **Grande Mosquée**, the symbol of Tiznit, which dates from the early 20th century. According to tradition, the perches which stick out from the tower are the resting place of souls; in reality they have a more practical function as supports for the painters putting on fresh whitewash. North of the mosque is the spring of Lalla Tiznit which, as legend has it, miraculously gushed forth when a pious reformed prostitute, Lalla Tiznit, was martyred. There is an interesting little souk on Thursdays supplying the population with their everyday needs: vegetables, spices, woven mats, two-handled baskets and colourful donkey saddles as well as silver jewellery.

Jewellery from Tiznit is well-known all over Morocco. **Place Kissaria des Bijoutiers** contains an astonishing number of shops selling Arabian gold jewellery from the cities and traditional Berber jewellery, both original articles and copies, and including the large, chased triangular clasps made of silver alloys with which the women of the region have fastened their garments since time immemorial.

High noon in Tleta Akhssass

Desert near Bouzakarne

53

South of Tiznit, the road climbs the western ridge of the Anti-Atlas and crosses the Tizi-Mighert, 1,057m (3,468ft) high. From here, when the weather conditions are right, there is a splendid view over the whole plateau. Shortly afterwards at a height of 1,000m (3,300ft), the road enters the little town of **Tleta Akhssass**. Here, the Tuesday souk specializes mainly in livestock.

Skirting the southern slopes of the western Anti-Atlas, with its rounded summits and sparse argan forests, the road descends to **Bouzakarne**, 158km (98 miles), at a height of 600m (2,000ft). Here too, the numerous new buildings are evidence of rapid growth in the busy town on this important Saharan road. The red-

Guelmim colours

dish-brown stony desert, stunted argan trees, thorny shrubs and grazing black goats everywhere are unmistakeable signs of the nearby Sahara.

The buildings of **Guelmim** (pop. 73,000), 199km (124 miles), the red gate to the Western Sahara, are almost the same colour as their surroundings. A crumbling kasbah is the symbol of the provincial capital. While it has lost its former importance as the main base of the caravan trade, its position on the major road from Tangier to Mauritania – the route used for the transportation of all essential goods into the up-and-coming towns of the Western Sahara and from the Saharan provinces to Agadir and Casablanca – guarantees it a role as a small trading centre and the intermediate destination of long-distance lorry drivers. The proximity of the desert is most evident around the reddish arcades of the old town. This is also where most of the 'blue men' are to be found. The well-known Guedra dancers of Guelmim have been reduced to the status of a tourist attraction, paid by travel firms and hotel managers.

Tafraoute: a unique setting

Detour to Tafraoute

An alternative route from Agadir to Tiznit involves a detour inland via Tafraoute and the Kerdous Pass (1,110m/3,642ft). This is one of the most exciting routes in Morocco and can be done as part of a round trip from Agadir. It passes first through the barren but impressive rocky landscape of the Anti-Atlas, snaking along the high edge of the mountains with dramatic views above and below. Cone-shaped outcrops of rock rear out of the valley floor, crowned by agadirs (fortified granaries) and farms. Nothing much grows here, but every so often there are isolated argan trees with goats searching among the branches for food; the occasional cluster of palms and white-domed *koubbas* lift the many shades of pink, ginger and brown.

Guide in Tafraoute

The high point of the tour is ★★ **Tafraoute** (pop. 4,000) in its unique setting. In this high Anti-Atlas valley, 1,000m (3,280ft) above sea level, erosion has created bizarre natural monuments out of boulders of pink granite, and against this backdrop the villagers have also painted their houses pink.

Tafraoute is particularly worth visiting in February at the time of the almond blossom, when it attracts crowds of tourists. The area is well worth exploring on foot, and guides will lead you to *Les Roches Bleus*, fauvist boulders painted shades of blue in the rockscape by the Belgian artist Jean Veran.

Nearby, in the idyllic valley of the Ammeln tribe, with its argan trees, the pink villages cling like birds' nests to the 2,359-m (7,740-ft) Jbel Lekst.

Route 9

A taste of the Atlas

Marrakech – Asni – Tizi-n-Test – Taroudannt – Agadir (304km/189 miles) *See map on page 52*

The moods and landscapes of the Atlas change with the seasons: in the spring there is a sea of apple, pear, almond and peach blossom, in the summer the summits are veiled in mist, in the autumn brightly attired Berber women stagger home with bundles of brushwood, and in the winter ice crystals glitter on the branches and smoke rises above the clay-walled houses of the mountain villages. The trip over the pass of Tizi-n-Test at a height of 2,092m (6,657ft) is an experience in every season. Until the early 20th century, the Goundafi Berbers controlled the traditional crossing from the Haouz Plateau in the north to the Vallée du Souss in the south, a passage feared by sultans and trading caravans alike, as it could easily be blocked off. Times, however, have changed and the buses carrying tourists, who are not so numerous in this part of Morocco, can cross the pass without paying a toll. The numerous kasbahs in the high valley of the Nfiss still testify to the former power of the Goundafi *caïds*, a Berber tribe that had a firm hold on this area. Looking down into the citrus valley in the southwest you can almost smell the orange groves which surround the town of Taroudannt.

Mount Toubkal in winter **55**

An overnight stay at Ouirgane and Taroudannt is recommended. The route takes two to three days. Drivers crossing the Tizi-n-Test should take care – the road narrows near the top and the hairpin bends can be extremely treacherous.

The first section of this route, the stretch from Marrakech (*see page 38*) to Tahanaoute, is characterised by olive groves. Forty percent of the country's olive production comes from more than 8 million olive trees in this region. The road bordered by eucalyptus trees runs through these groves in the direction of the High Atlas. In the local administrative centre of **Tahanaoute** (34km/21 miles), at a height of 995m (3,264ft), a traditional market is held every Tuesday.

Berber woman

Mount of olives

Even more unspoilt is the souk in the high mountain town of **Asni** (1,150m/3,773ft) on the left bank of the Asif Reraïa. However, the livestock and corn market is not the sole attraction of this little town: it is also splendidly located with impressive views of the nearby summits of the High Atlas. It is very popular as a summer resort, especially with the people of Marrakech. From

Asni it is possible to take a detour to the village of **Imlil**, 17km (10 miles) away (the road deteriorates after 12 km/7 miles, but it can be tackled in a small car). Lying at the foot of **Mont Toubkal**, the highest peak in North Africa (4,167m/13,670ft), Imlil is the main springboard for hiking expeditions into the Toubkal massif and from early summer through to autumn throngs with hikers, mules and guides.

After leaving Asni the road continues to climb. The peaceful hotel of La Roseraie is recommended (*see page 102*) if you want to benefit from the mountain air for a little longer. The hotel organises rides on pedigree horses to the holm oak woods, and every Thursday there is a souk in the nearby village of **Ouirgane** at a height of 1,000m (3,300 ft).

High Atlas scenery

The narrow high **Vallée du Nfiss** with its junipers is a fascinating place where the mountainsides, river banks and steep cliffs are studded with clay-walled villages and kasbahs. The area is a particular delight for hikers. The village of **Ijoukak**, 94km (58 miles), at a height of 1,185m (3,888ft), is a starting point for mountain tours.

The Nfiss was the stronghold of the powerful Goundafi tribe, and to the left of the road after Ijoukak there is a Goundafi kasbah. The fortresses of the High Atlas differ both in appearance and function from the kasbahs of the Draâ and Dadès valleys. They were built by powerful tribal leaders at strategic points to control the problematic passes and were power symbols marking the domains of the various *caïds*. By the end of the 19th century Tayeb el Goundafi, one of the three principal lords of the Atlas, could raise an army of 5,000 men.

The mosque at Tin-Mal

A little further on (1 km/½mile), the road climbs via the Oued Nfiss to the historic site of ★ **Tin-Mal** at a height of 1,200m (3,937ft), dominated by the Almohad mosque. The rise and importance of the Almohads is closely associated with the name of Mohammed Ibn Abdallah Ibn Toumert, who was born in 1080 and went down in history as a religious fanatic. As a politically dangerous agitator, he was banned from Marrakech and settled in Tin-Mal, where he continued to defend his interpretation of the Koran. Of the mountain fortress founded in 1125 only traces of the walls remain. Abd el-Moumen (113–63), his successor, ruled over the most powerful realm in the Arabic West, which stretched from the united Morocco to Tripolitania and included Al-Andalus. After the Merinids took over, the last Almohads retired to Tin-Mal, but were unable to prevent the destruction of their *ribat*.

The grande mosque fell into ruin, although it was the model for important sacred buildings such as the

Mural in Taroudannt

Koutoubia in Marrakech (*see page 39*). It was not until 1991–92 that it was restored, and now the local people gather here for Friday prayers. The richly decorated prayer niche, the *mihrab*, ranks as a masterpiece of Almohad art.

Further along the road, the Goundafi kasbah of **Tagoundaft**, built in 1865 at a height of 1,600m (5,249ft), comes into view.

From Idni onwards, the road passes through the Nfiss gorge and spirals up to the ★ **Tizi-n-Test**. From the top of the pass (2,092m/6,863ft) there is a magnificent view of the wide Vallée du Souss, 200km (124 miles) long and separating the High and the Anti-Atlas.

The southern side of the Atlas is much more barren than the north. Thorny argan trees take over the vegetation in an otherwise desolate landscape. Occasionally a quilt of green fields stitched round a few oases brightens the monotony.

But down in the valley of the Chleuh Berbers the orange and olive groves stretch to Agadir. At Aït-Yazza a 24-km (15-mile) detour can be made to **Tiouate**. This oasis with its spring is dominated by an old kasbah, the former residence of the *caïd* Mohammed Tiouti.

★ **Taroudannt** (pop. 57,000), 223km (139 miles), is set spectacularly against the backdrop of the Atlas Mountains, which in the winter are covered in snow. Its pale red city wall was built under the regency of Moulay Ismaïl. The high clay wall has five gates and still almost surrounds the whole town.

In the 16th century, Taroudannt enjoyed a brief reputation as the capital of the Saadians. Today, it is the capital of the province of the same name. The main squares of the medina, Place Al-Alaouyine, Place Talmeklat and Place Jotia with their craft shops are full of local colour. They are also the location of cheap hotels and cafés.

57

An ancient find

The wall of Taroudannt

Melons galore

Route 10

Morocco in green

Rabat

Surfeit of sunflowers

Casablanca – Rabat – Kénitra – Rharb – Larache – Asilah – Tangier (372km) *See map on pages 60–61*

Morocco, traditionally pictured as the land of the kasbahs and bare mountains, is not usually thought of as a green country. However, along the Atlantic coastal flats are extensive orange, sugarbeet and sugar cane plantations, green carpets of peanut fields and in August thousands of sunflowers turning their plate-sized heads towards the sun. First, however, the road passes through the largest conurbation in Morocco: the cosmopolitan Casablanca, followed by the small, introspective administrative city of Rabat, then Kénitra set in the midst of flat countryside. Finally, in the far north, Tangier flings open its doors to Europe.

Two to three days should be allowed for this route. Between Casablanca (*see page 22*) and Rabat there is actually a choice of three roads. The narrow coastal road runs past the beaches, but if you are short of time take the new motorway, for which there is a toll. This is being extended to Tangier. The old inland road runs through towns such as Bouznika, Skhirat and Témara, with side roads branching off to the beaches, which in the summer are very crowded.

In high summer there is heavy traffic on the coast road, as many of the local people have holiday homes by the beaches. After the drab industrial suburbs of Casablanca, the palm-lined avenues of the harbour town of **Mohammedia**, 28km (17 miles), make a refreshing change. There is some pollution from nearby oil refineries and petrochemicals plants, but the daytrippers who flock to Mohammedia from Casablanca are evidently not put off by this. They turn the beach into their summer playground, and come here to play golf and watch the horse-racing.

About 11km (7 miles) before Rabat is the **Parc Zoologique National de Rabat** (daily 10am– 5.30pm). In addition to Barbary apes and dromedaries, the 50-hectare (124-acre) zoo has several Atlas lions, which can no longer be found in the wild.

The section of the motorway from Rabat (*see page 16*) to Kénitra crosses the Forêt de la Mamora (*see page 67*) with its cork oaks, acacias and eucalyptus trees, but there is more to see on the old road close to the coast.

Cork in the Forêt de la Mamora

Nine kilometres (6 miles) north of Salé is the **Jardin Exotique de Rabat-Salé** (daily 10am–5.30pm). These botanical gardens were laid out during the protectorate by the Frenchman M. François and occupy an area of 4 hectares (10 acres). The complex has been rather neglected and in the course of time become a jungle that can only be negotiated on marked paths: the walk round is an adventure that will delight both adults and children.

The detour via Mehdiya-Plage follows side roads round the southern tip of the **Lac Sidi-Bourhaba**. This 600-hectare (1,500-acre) wetland area is protected by the Ramsar Convention (international convention for the protection of wetlands as an environment for waders and water birds). The nearby **Mehdiya-Plage** on the estuary of the Sebou river is a local recreation area. The ruined kasbah, high above the outer harbour, was built at the end of the 17th century by Moulay Ismaïl to control the navigable estuary.

Kénitra (pop. 292,000), 133km (83 miles), capital of the province of the same name, is located on a bend of the Sebou and has the only inland harbour in Morocco. The main products shipped from here are ores, molasses and paper. Built by the French in 1913, it is a typical colonial town with shady avenues lined with plane trees, but has no tourist attractions worthy of note.

The **Rharb**, Morocco's modern, technologically advanced agricultural area, has a surprising number of water towers and irrigation channels. The fertile alluvial soil is ideal for growing early vegetables for export, oil plants for the production of cooking oil, cereals, sugar cane and sugarbeet. There are also large cattle and sheep farms. **Souk-el-Arba-du-Rharb**, 211km (131 miles), is a good place for a refreshment break. A popular stopping place for long-distance lorries, cars and buses, it

Orchards in the Rharb

has simple restaurants on both sides of the through road serving tasty, freshly-fried tender lamb chops. The souk held every Wednesday is an important regional market.

On the Spanish-looking Place de la Libération of **Larache** (pop. 90,000), 284km (176 miles), which most tourists drive through on their way to nearby Lixus (*see below*), are a number of pleasant terrace cafés and restaurants ideal for a break. From this square there are roads to the new town as well as to the medina with the Bab el-Khemis and the souk. Winding alleys lead to the **Musée Archéologique**, in the former palace of Sultan Youssef Abdelhak el-Merini (1258–81), displaying ancient artefacts and a collection of coins.

★ **Lixus** is the second most important excavation site in Morocco after Volubilis. Originally founded by the Phoenicians in about 1100BC, from AD40 to the 5th century it was a thriving Roman trading centre. With 10 fish-salting establishments, it was the largest salting centre in the colony of Mauretania Tingitana. On the left-hand side of the road are the foundation walls of the 147 basins where salted fish and garum paste from anchovies were produced for Rome. A footpath leads up onto the hill platform and the ruins of the upper town, in which rows of seats from the amphitheatre and temple foundations have been excavated. In the baths next to the theatre, there is a beautiful floor mosaic with the expressive head of Oceanus, the god of the sea. Many of the floor

Salt works at Larache

60

Excavations at Lixus

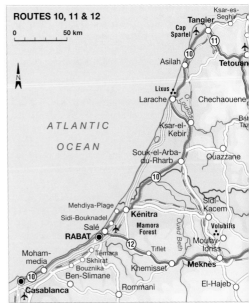

ROUTES 10, 11 & 12

0   50 km

N

Ksar-es-Seghir
Tangier
Cap Spartel
Asilah
Tetouan
Chechaouene
Lixus
Larache
Bab Taz
Ksar-el-Kebir
Souk-el-Arba-du-Rharb
Ouazzane
ATLANTIC OCEAN
Mehdiya-Plage
Sidi-Bouknadel
Salé
Kénitra
Mamora Forest
RABAT
Sidi Kacem
Volubilis
Moulay Idriss
Tiflèt
Oued Beth
Meknès
Moham-media
Témara
Skhirat
Bouznika
Ben-Slimane
Khemisset
Rommani
El-Hajeb
Casablanca
Oued Loukos

mosaics from the merchants' houses heve been removed and transferred to the museum in Tetouan (*see page 63*).

Although little has remained of ancient Lixus, its location controlling the estuary and the hinterland of the Oued Loukos is impressive. It was this fertile plain that the ancient Greeks believed to be the site of the gardens of the Hesperides, where the mythical golden apples grew that gave those who ate them immortality and eternal youth. Lixus is also supposed to be the place where Hercules won a wrestling match with the Libyan giant Anteus, the mythical founder of the city of Tangier.

The little town of **Asilah** (pop. 25,000), 325km (202 miles), with its beautiful beaches, attracts many Moroccan and foreign visitors. An international culture festival is usually held here in August and during the 10-day *moussem* (*see page 85*) the few hotel rooms are booked out. The development of an appropriate infrastructure has been shamefully neglected since the founding of the festival in 1978, but plans are now afoot to change all this and Asilah is even to have a marina for the convenience of its boat-owning visitors. In the Palais de la Culture and the Centre Hassan II, international music and dance groups perform and on the Place Al Kmrah the Gnaoua beat their drums and rattle their castanets. The Thursday souk is particularly picturesque and the Portuguese wall conceals a charming old town centre.

Modern art in Asilah

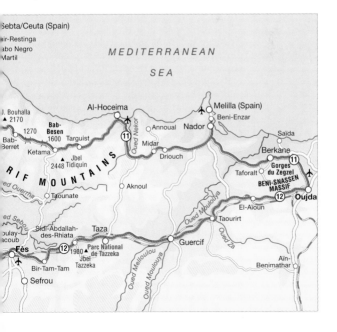

The Rif's red slopes

Route 11

The Rif Mountains

Tangier – Tetouan – Chechaouèn – Al-Hoceima – Oujda (628km/390 miles) *See map on pages 60–61*

The N2 boldly sweeps over passes, reaching 1,600m (5,250ft) at its highest point. To the east cork oaks, cedars and pines accentuate the green, which in winter lies hidden under a glittering mantle of snow. There are few houses on the red slopes, and mule paths wind up to isolated farms. As well as its beautiful scenery, the Rif is well known for growing Indian hemp, commonly known as marijuana, which thrives hidden amongst the maize fields. For some time the government has been vigorously promoting its replacement with other crops. In addition, a large security force operates in the region to combat illegal drug dealing. You are strongly advised against buying hashish (kif), the narcotic drug derived from the plant. If you are caught with the substance you could be imprisoned for up to five years.

With overnight stops in Tetouan, Chechaouèn and Al-Hoceima the route takes four days by car.

Aspects of Tetouan

From Tangier (*see page 44*) it is only 57km (35 miles) to ★ **Tetouan** (pop. 280,000). In the summer the town is a stopping-off point for many expatriate Moroccans on their way back home via Ceuta and Tangier for a holiday. In the most popular resorts by the sea there is a shortage of beds in the season and a noticeable rise in the noise level. There is also constant through traffic to the beaches of Martil, Cabo Negro, Mdiq and Smir-Restinga and their holiday complexes.

No other Ville Nouvelle in northern Morocco has such pronounced Spanish features as Tetouan, the former administrative centre of the occupying power. The part that is most fascinating for tourists is the medina, founded in the 16th century by refugees from Al-Andalus. With its numerous mosques, shrines, decorative portals, wall fountains, vaulted passages and steep flights of steps, the old town has a character all of its own, enlivened by the colourful souks with their wide range of genuine craft products. The **Musée de l'Ethnographie** by the Bab el-Okla has a comprehensive collection of the region's arts and crafts. And the **Musée Archéologique**, (2 Rue Ibn Hsaïn, Ville Nouvelle; 9am–noon, 2.30–5.30pm; closed Tuesday) has findings from the Roman towns, including the beautiful mosaic floors transferred from Lixus (*see pages 60–61*).

Past glories recalled

★★ Chechaouene (pop. 31,000), 121km (75 miles), describes itself in superlatives as the most beautifully located, attractive and romantic town in the Rif. At a height of 520–760m (1,700–2,500ft), it is dominated by steep, 2,000-m (6,000-ft) mountains. Chechaouene was founded in 1471 by Reconquista refugees from Al-Andalus under the leadership of Moulay Ali Ben Rachid, whose mausoleum still attracts pilgrims. Until it was taken by the Spaniards in 1920, Christians were not allowed to enter this pilgrimage town. When they did, they discovered a community of Jews, descended from the first refugee settlers, speaking 10th-century Castilian, a language extinct in Spain for over 400 years, and leather craftsmen working in tanned and decorated leather as their ancestors had done in 12th-century Cordoba.

Chechaouene: fountain detail

63

Today, Chechaouene lives from the pilgrims, tourism and the sale of craft products. A fountain plays on the Outa el-Hammam, the main square of the old town, and the street cafés are shaded by mulberry trees. On the southeast side of the square is the **Grande Mosquée**, one of the town's first buildings: only its octagonal minaret dates from a later period. The kasbah, from which there is a splendid panoramic view, was built by Moulay Ismaïl. The Jebala Berber women wearing broad-brimmed bast hats and straight red-and-white striped skirts are dominant figures at the market held every Monday and Thursday.

Shady courtyard

Small, expanding market towns such as Bab-Taza, Bab-Berret or Bab-Besen lie along the pass road as it climbs to the magnificent cedar forest in the vicinity of **Ketama**. This town is set in the midst of the largest hemp-growing area in Morocco, but it is also a well-known winter sports resort and starting point for excursions to the **Tidiquin Massif** (2,448m/8,031ft).

On the beach at Al-Hoceima

Through mountains red as the setting sun the road spirals down to **Al-Hoceima** (pop. 55,000) on the Mediterranean coast, 334km (208 miles). The beaches and small rocky bays are particularly popular with Moroccans and Spaniards but out of season it is quiet here.

Heading inland again, the road winds uphill along the Nekor valley, where the crops grow green in the fertile soil of the wide river bed. The new settlements that have grown up around the old market sites such as Midar or Driouch have few attractions, and **Nador** (pop. 112,000), 488km (303 miles), the provincial capital on the lagoon of Sebka bou Areq, also has no sights of cultural interest. The enlargement of the harbour of Beni-Enzar is proceeding apace to take some of the traffic away from nearby Melilla. Further east, in the alluvial plain of the Oued Moulouya, in the midst of large orange groves, is the agricultural centre of **Berkane**, which is also the source of the good Beni-Snassen wines.

To the south of Berkane it is possible to make a detour into the **Beni-Snassen Massif**, which rises to a height of 1,532m (5,026ft). The porous limestone mountains were named after the powerful Berber tribe that had already settled here before the spread of Islam. There are two caves to visit: in the prehistoric **Grotte du Pigeon** (Dove Grotto) two necropolises were found with 180 skeletons of the early *homo sapiens sapiens*, from the period between the 20th and the 8th millennia BC. The **Grotte du Chameau** is named after the stalagmite in the shape of a camel at the entrance.

Taking the plunge in the Gorges du Zegzel

This round trip of 138km (86 miles) also passes through the scattered village of **Sidi-Bouhria**, the mountain village of **Taforalt** and the rust-red, richly cultivated ★ **Gorges du Zegzel**, before returning to Berkane. If possible, plan the excursion on a Wednesday so that you can visit the souk in Taforalt.

Ahfir, 591km (367 miles), is one of the Algerian border points that is currently closed. It is only a short hop of 20km (12 miles) from here to **Saïdia**, a crowded summer resort on the Mediterrean coast with a wide sandy beach. Our route however continues south along the border and ends in **Oujda** (pop.350,000), 628km (390 miles), the most important town in eastern Morocco, next to the Algerian border. Having been fought over for centuries by Berbers, Arabs and Turks, peace finally came to Oujda in 1907 when it was occupied by the French. The town has no important architectural monuments, but a stroll through the street of the jewellers, El-Mazouzi, and the souks to the Bab Sidi Abd el Ouahab on the east side of the city wall is highly recommended.

Oujda outpost

Route 12

Kasbah along the Sultans' Road

The Sultans' Road

Oujda – Fès – Meknès – Rabat (550km/342 miles)
See map on pages 60–61

65

Even the Romans were afraid of the Taza Plain, the narrow corridor parallel to the Rif and Middle Atlas. For centuries Berber tribes from the neighbouring mountain regions caused disturbances here and not without reason: all the invaders from the east used this relatively easy passage on their campaigns of conquest. The area is still strategically important and there are heavy concentrations of Moroccan military forces here. The scenery is pastoral: steppe with grazing sheep, silvery olive groves and the citrus fruits of the Sebou basin. The high points of this route are the old sultan capitals of Fès, Meknès and Rabat with their world-famous Moorish architecture (each covered in earlier chapters). Nevertheless, there is plenty to interest the visitor between the cities. With overnight stays in Taza, Fès (two nights) and Meknès, five days should be allowed for the car journey.

Sheep on the steppe

The grey ribbon of asphalt runs in almost a straight line across the plain. The young olive groves and pinewoods are evidence of the government's determination to reforest the barren land. The kasbahs – many of them built by Moulay Ismaïl in the 17th century – are relics of armed conflict and plunder. On the Sultans' Road, as it is called today for the benefit of the tourists, Berbers from the Beni-Snassen tribe uesd to lie in wait for the trade caravans.

Beautiful maple trees grow along the streets of the administrative town of **El-Aïoun**, 59km (37 miles). The

Hot spice in Taourirt

Taza toddler and Moorish detail

Tuesday souk is visited by representatives of many different Berber tribes. El-Aïoun has a military kasbah with a mosque built during the reign of Moulay Ismaïl.

Splendid gleditsias meet across the road into the new town of **Taourirt**, and pepper trees line the streets. Until the early 20th century the original town, 5km (3 miles) to the northwest, was contained within the walls of the kasbah, which was built by Moulay Ismaïl on a junction of the caravan routes from Sijilmassa in the Tafilalt to Melilla and from the east to the Maghreb.

On the vast, barren steppe graze the sheep of the Haouara tribe. The countryside only becomes green again in the vicinity of **Guercif**, 162km (101 miles), on the Oued Moulouya.

Taza (pop. 120,000), 227km (141 miles), is the administrative centre of the province of the same name. For centuries it was an unwritten rule that it was only possession of Taza, and with it the important east-west passage, that guaranteed control over Fès. So it is not surprising that this former fortified monastery built by the Meknassa Berbers was already being fought over in the 10th century by the power-hungry dynasties. In 1914 the French established a garrison on the plateau below the old town and from here master-minded the defeat of the Rif rebellion (*see page 13*).

The drab new town, situated approximately 2km (1½ miles) northeast of the old town, has little in the way of tourist attractions. By contrast the medina, at a height of 580m (1,903ft), is still surrounded by a wall and has original religious 12th-century buildings from the Almohad era. Visitors usually begin their tour of the medina at the Bab Jemaa on the east side and thus come onto the Rue Nejjarine, the south-north artery of the old town, with its tempting jewellery and cloth shops. Continue past the Mausolée de Sidi Azouz, the patron of Taza, with an Almohad minaret and Moorish wall fountain, to the Grande Mosquée on the northern edge of the medina with its prominent Almohad minaret. From the Bab er-Rih in the northern wall there is a fine view of the lower town in its olive-green setting.

After Taza a detour of 76km (47 miles) can be made through the ★ **Parc National de Tazzeka**. This is undoubtedly the most impressive section of this otherwise scenically rather monotonous route. The 12,700-hectare (31,400-acre) national park is home to wild pigs, jackals, red foxes, red deer and diurnal and nocturnal birds of prey. The magnificent cedar forest on the **Jbel Tazzeka** (1,980m/6,260ft) is a protected area. And even though you will probably not see any animals, the trip itself is extremely worthwhile. Cork, holm, turkey and

Places: Route 12

kermes oaks, thujas and oleanders cover the slopes. Although the **Grottes du Chiker** (1,344m/4,409ft) cannot be visited, you can take a look inside the **Gouffre de Friouato** (1,492m /4,895ft), a dripstone cave explored to a depth of 305m (1,001ft) and length of 2,221m (7,287ft). Only the top section can be visited in the company of a watchman, who takes you down the 512 steps to a depth of 180m (591ft).

After you have traversed the passes of Bab-Bou-Idir (1,540m/5,052ft) and Bab-Taka (1,459m/4,786ft), a wooded road branches off to the summit of Jbel Tazzeka. In winter this stretch is frequently unpassable and even in the summer it is often only negotiable with a four-wheel drive. Continue down through dense cork oak forests, and the winding Oued Zireg gorge, 10km (6 miles) long, to rejoin the main road at the scattered settlement of Sidi-Abdallah-des-Rhiata.

As the road rises towards the Bir-Tam-Tam (578m/ 1,896ft), 304km (189 miles), there is a view of the massive **Idriss I reservoir** on the Oued Sebou. Cereals, citrus fruits and olives thrive in the rich black soil of the area. The road then spirals down into the Sebou basin where Morocco's cultural centre Fès (*see page 32*) lies at a height of 415m (1,362ft).

The plateau between the two great cities of Fès and Meknès is predominantly agricultural. At midday a rest is in order: along the main roads running through the small market towns are places to stop for tender charcoal-grilled lamb. The Ismaïl city of **Meknès** (*see page 26*) is already visible from a long way off.

Yellow and mauve flowers carpet the sunny hills on the far side of Meknès in the spring. These slopes also produce the best grapes in Morocco.

Khemisset (pop. 100,000) is the rapidly growing capital of the province of the same name. This agricultural centre in the territory of the Zemmour Berbers has made a name for itself due to its fine carpets. The numerous street cafés under the arcades are a pleasant place to break your journey.

After **Tiflèt**, 494km (307 miles), the route takes you through the largest cork oak forest in Morocco, the **Forêt de la Mamora**, a sandy area measuring 60 by 40km (37 by 25 miles) in which pines have also been planted. The trees are interspersed with mimosa: in March and April their brightly coloured flowers turn the area a vivid yellow that make it visible for miles. The road finally crosses the Pont Hassan II with a view of the mausoleum, illuminated at night, to enter the capital of **Rabat**, 550km (342 miles) (*see page 16*).

Gouffre de Friouato

Gorge in the Jbel Tazzeka

Negotiating the Erg Chebbi

Rabat

Date palms near Erfoud

Route 13

Into the desert

Fès – Ifrane – Azrou – Er Rachidia – Erg Chebbi – Rissani (478km/297 miles) *See map on page 76*

The contrasts along this route could hardly be greater. After the winter sports resorts of the Middle Atlas such as Imouzzèr or Ifrane, which bear certain resemblances to their counterparts in central Europe, the scene begins to change at Midelt in the northeastern part of the High Atlas. On the way south, the green date-palm oases of the Tafilalt contrast with spreading cedar forests and clay-walled villages built to resist invaders, and the trans-Atlas tour culminates spectacularly in the reddish-golden dunes of the Erg Chebbi.

For the Fès–Rissani route at least two days are necessary, including stops.

Only 38km (24 miles) from Fès (*see page 32*), at a height of 1,350m (4,429ft) is the health resort of **Imouzzèr-du-Kandar**, in the shadow of the 1,768-m (5,801-ft) summit of the same name. Apple and pear trees flourish in this rainy part of the Middle Atlas. The whole area with its holiday complexes is popular both summer and winter with the wealthy middle classes from Casablanca, Fès, Meknès and Rabat.

Situated at a height of 1,650m (5,413ft), **Ifrane**, 63km (39 miles), is rather more chic, which is not solely due to the splendid hunting lodge belonging to King Hassan that stands in the cedar forest. Pompous, red-tiled villas and chalets belonging to well-off Moroccans are concealed in large gardens.

Ifrane was founded in 1929 by French settlers who, during the protectorate, owned large estates in the triangle formed by Meknès, Fès and Ifrane. This was their leisure paradise, where they came to ski, hunt and fish. Today, Ifrane is the administrative centre of the province of the same name and is the most popular skiing area next to Oukaïmeden (*see page 43*). The excellent slopes lie 17km (11 miles) to the south on the Mischliffen (2,036m/6,680ft) and the Jbel Hebri (2,104m/6,903ft). In 1994 the university of Al-Akhawayn was opened, which was founded at the instigation of the King, and modelled on American colleges. To cater for the three monotheistic religions, a mosque, a synagogue and a church were built on the campus: they stand as symbols of the 'tolerant Islam' promoted by King Hassan.

Azrou (pop. 41,000), at a height of 1,250m (4,100ft), is an important market centre for the Beni-Mguild Berbers, who inhabit a large area in the central Middle Atlas. Some of them still live a semi-nomadic life with their dark-brown tents. As you approach the town from the north, the green-tiled minaret of the Mosquée Hassan I is the first thing that comes into view; the green tiles are also to be found on some of the houses, and are a characteristic feature of Moorish architecture. In the western part of town was the kasbah, built in the 17th century, although little remains of it now. At the centre is the volcanic outcrop from which Azrou gets its name. Here, painted on in Arabic script, are the three determining elements in the life of every Moroccan: God (top), nation (right) and king (left).

Azrou local

69

Azrou is famous for its sheep's-wool carpets and cedarwood carvings. These products are for sale in the Coopérative Artisanale. You can also visit a carpet-knotting factory.

Carpet in production

Past the rough-stone houses of **Timahdite** (1,815m/ 5,958ft), a place that is popular with mountaineers, the route continues across a high plateau of volcanic origin with the Col du Zad, at 2,178m (7,146ft), marking its highest point.

From Aït-Oufella onwards, (155km/96 miles), the view to the south is dominated by the towering ramparts of the 3,737-m (12,260-ft) Jbel Ayachi; for months its long ridge is covered in snow. The town of **Midelt** (pop. 39,000), 205 km (127 miles), at a height of 1,488m (4,882ft), is also an ideal climatic health resort as well as a popular destination for mineral collectors.

It is only after the Tagalm Pass (1,907m/6,257ft) that the road starts its descent down the bare lee side of the High Atlas onto the high plateau of the pre-Sahara. After the

Kasbah in the Vallée du Ziz

70

Window detail

little town of Rich, the road follows the winding course of the desert river Ziz, running through the spectacular ★ **Gorges du Ziz**. The red cliffs, argan trees, tamarisks, palms, rich green fields and clay-built villages on the river banks make this a very picturesque area indeed.

The route continues past the Barrage (dam) Hassan-Addakhil to **Er-Rachidia** (pop. 62,000), 346km (215 miles). Some visitors are pleasantly surprised, others disappointed by this town, but eventually everyone succumbs to its unique fascination. Maybe it is the natural illuminative effects of the setting sun, which turn the simple red house facades a rich purple; it is at sunset that the shop owners also open their doors after the long siesta. Perhaps it is also the souk on Tuesdays, Thursdays and Sundays, where the inhabitants of the nearby oases sell their products. Or is it the pre-Saharan atmosphere that puts you in such a questing, anticipative mood? Realistically, the town has nothing special to offer. It developed as the location of a French garrison, which was stationed here at a height of 1,060m (3,478ft) on a strategic junction of the major roads from the Atlantic to Algeria and from central Morocco to the Sahara Desert.

The main road now runs along the Vallée du Ziz parallel to oases with thousands of date palms. The route is lined with the clay-coloured *ksour* (*see page 81*) typical of the region. Such villages, a common sight in Morocco, are surrounded by a protective wall with fortified towers up to 12m (39ft) high, with a main gate, also flanked by towers, and a labyrinth of alleyways inside. Only 2km (1 mile) after **Maadid**, water fountains jet into the sky not far from the road. In search of drinking water, American geologists only found slightly salty water, which, although it cannot be used for irrigating the fields, is pumped along pipelines to serve households in the pre-Saharan towns of Erfoud and Rissani.

Erfoud (pop. 18,000), 425km (264 miles), was also originally a garrison, established by the French in 1917 to control the nearby border territory. The Tafilalt was once the main trading centre for the trade caravans in southeast Morocco. Today the inhabitants live from oasis farming, breeding sheep, and tourism. If you want to buy fossils, but do not want to hunt for them yourself, you will find some fine specimens at the Sahara-Sea-Collection, opposite the Hotel Tafilalet on the main road through town.

Erfoud market

Erfoud is the main base for trips to the dramatic sand dunes of ★★ **Erg Chebbi**, the highest in Morocco (up to 100m/328ft). It is worth spending at least one night in one of the simple hotels beneath the dunes or in a tent, as only then will you have the opportunity to experience the sight of the magnificent play of colours across the sand at sunrise and sunset.

The road to Erg Chebbi is tarmac for 17km (11 miles) becoming a track for a further 36km (22 miles), culminating in the oasis of **Merzouga**. Visitors may prefer to negotiate the myriad tracks with the help of a guide, easily hired in Erfoud or Rissani. However, orientation is easy once you see the glowing red dunes in the distance, contrasted against the grey and brown stony desert of the approach. Although small in size compared to the dunes of the Sahara proper, once you are in it, the Erg Chebbi does give something of the feeling of endless desert; reason enough for it to have been used as a location of a number of films, including *Lawrence of Arabia*.

The dunes from Merzouga

As well as climbing the dunes, visitors to Merzouga can walk around the village, meet the locals and check out the **Depot Nomade**, whose proprietor explains the various patterns of the Berber carpets on sale. There is little pressurised salesmanship here, and the prices are fair – a refreshing change from most such outlets in Morocco.

Berber patterns at Merzouga's Depot Nomade

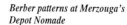

A few hundred metres outside **Rissani**, the red clay walls of the legendary trading town of Sijilmassa rise out of the sand. Until the 14th century, it was a checkpoint for the caravans passing through to the just as legendary Tombouctou. When Rissani took over as the main town of the Tafilalt, Sijilmassa gradually disappeared beneath the sand; excavation work on this site has now been in progress since 1996. On Tuesdays, Thursdays and Sundays, the souk of Rissani is a focal point for tourists, where under the arcades Berber women dressed in dark robes sell beautiful jewellery.

The old ksar in Goulmina

Rabat

Kasbah dweller

Oasis along the Dadès

Route 14

Valley of a thousand kasbahs

Erfoud – Gorges du Todra – Gorges du Dadès – El-Kelaâ M'Gouna – Skoura – Ouarzazate (311km/193 miles) *See map on page 76*

Painters and photographers will be equally fascinated by the harmony of colours and forms along this route: on one side the High Atlas with its jagged, often snow-capped peaks rising to between 3,000–4,000m (10,000–13,000ft); on the other the dramatic but much more barren 2,500-m (8,000-ft) summits of the Jbel Sarhro. And cutting into the Atlas, the famous Todra and Dadès gorges. Along the main valley and part way into the gorges, numerous oases line the rather dry river courses. Red clay *ksour* (*see page 81*) blend into river terraces of the same colour; defiant kasbahs with high towers catch the eye. By the late autumn, the snow-white ridges of the mountains are already sharply defined against the deep blue sky. In the evening, the kasbahs glow red above silvery rivers. Beauty and exoticness have made the 'Valley of a Thousand Kasbahs' the classical route for every Morocco traveller.

Overnight stays in Tinerhir, Boumalne or El-Kelaâ M'Gouna are recommended. Two to three days should be allowed for this route.

Immediately to the west of Erfoud (*see page 71*) are the first oases with their old, half-ruined clay villages and castles. On the other side of Jorf, the otherwise flat desert plateau is studded with huge, molehill-like mounds, each of which conceals entrances to the ancient rhettaras, the irrigation channels which, fed from the ground water, supplied the oases with fresh water until they became completely sanded up. After the disastrous drought years of 1994–5, the oasis farmers remembered their pipelines and dug some of them out of the sand.

In **Tinejdad** the route joins the so-called Road of Kasbahs, which runs from Er-Rachidia to Ouarzazate. Tinejdad is the administrative centre of the Ferkla oases. **Asrir**, 5km (3 miles), a *ksar* (*see page 81*) west of the Municipalité du Tinejdad, is without a doubt one of the most interesting sights in the area. The women, mostly Haratines, wrap themselves in blue-black *haïks* decorated with colourful embroidery.

Goulmima ksar tower

A detour of 24km (15 miles) each way can be made to **Goulmima**, north of Tinejdad on the Oued Rheris. The old Goulmima *ksar*, 1.5km (1 mile) east of the town, has been restored and has an impressive main gate 14m (46ft) deep with three turns in it, flanked by high towers.

Halfway between Erfoud and Ouarzazate is **Tinerhir**. Situated near the mouth of the Gorges du Todra at a height of 1,342m (4,402ft), this is the administrative centre for the 72 *ksour* in the area. Tinerhir has the most important market and is very prosperous, being a particularly popular domicile for Moroccans returning from abroad. The souk is held every Monday, but on any day of the week the local produce can be sampled at the simple restaurants around the central market square: you simply order what you want from a butcher and grocer and it is cooked up for you on a barbecue. The oases around Tinerhir are inviting places to stop. Here, Aït-Atta Berbers, Chorfa Arabs, Haratines and other tribes eke out a living primarily from oasis farming, growing dates, olives, almonds, figs, pomegranates and grapes.

73

Tinerhir is the starting point for an interesting detour into the impressive scenery of the ★ **Gorges du Todra**. After approximately 13km (8 miles) you come to the narrow entry, only 10m (33ft) wide, dominated on either side by soaring, 300-m (980-ft) cliffs. If you are lucky, you may see a number of climbers inching their way up the walls. If you are unlucky, you may arrive in a longer rainy period or a shower when the water is knee-deep and you will be glad if you are driving a four-wheel drive. Be that as it may, the Todra is on the tour-bus route, so you may get stuck behind one as you drive through. The gorge itself is only about half a mile long; beyond it, a track leads via the village of Tamtattouchte into the inner sanctums of the Atlas Mountains. This track can only be negotiated by four-wheel drive and links up, via various high passes, with the Gorges du Dadès. In winter

The entrance to the Todra

The High Atlas above the Gorges du Dadès

Modern Boumalne

Contrasts in the Vallée du Dadès

this road is often icy and closed, in the spring after heavy rainfalls it is often flooded.

The main route continues from Tinerhir past the dominating kasbahs of **Imiter**, 176km (109 miles) through spectacular mountain scenery with the Atlas range in the north and the Jbel Sarhro in the south.

Boumalne, 195km (121 miles), on the Dadès river, is the modern administrative centre of the region and an important market town. On Wednesdays there is a lively souk attended by highland Berbers from the surrounding *ksour* who ride down on their donkeys.

The old Boumalne *ksar* has several massive kasbahs, most of which, however, have been deserted by their owners, who have built themselves comfortable new homes close by. These modern cement houses have, of course, completely spoiled the look of the place, but the prosperous heirs see this simply as 'progress'.

Boumalne is the starting point for a detour to the ★★ **Gorges du Dadès**. This canyon, around 33km (21 miles) long, has old *ksours* such as Aït-Ouffli, Aït-Arbi and Aït-Tamlalt, and is one of those rare places where there is almost perfect harmony between nature and architecture. With ochre-coloured walls, green valley bottoms and the snow-capped Atlas as a backdrop, the scenery here is impressive indeed.

The settled part of the gorge is much longer than the Todra, but unless you have a four-wheel drive vehicle, the end point of the route will probably be at the top of the steep-sided ravine, which is surmounted via a series of terrifying switchbacks.

The main route to the west continues down the ★★ **Vallée du Dadès**. On brownish-red outcrops are *ksour* of the same colour, which look even more massive but at the same time more beautiful as they glow in the light of the setting sun. On the last part of the route, *ksour* and kasbahs follow one another at short intervals. **El-Kelaâ M'Gouna**, 219km (136 miles), attracts many visitors in May with its rose festival (*see page 84*), featuring processions, dances and the election of a rose queen.

At a height of 1,467m (4,813ft) there are no more date palms, but a wide variety of fruit is grown as well as roses for the French perfume industry. On a cliff on the Asfi-M'Goun bank is a kasbah owned by the former *pacha* of Marrakech, Thami el-Glaoui. **Mont M'Goun** (4,071m/13,356ft), the second-highest peak in Morocco, rises awesomely to the north.

Skoura ksar and detail

The rose plantations extend as far as **Skoura**. In addition to date palms, argan, apple, almond and fig trees also thrive here. There are around 50 *ksour* scattered among the oases. A number of the many Skoura kasbahs have two unusual features: the corner towers are of differing height and width, and the upper parts of the towers are decorated with unusually lavish brick ornamentation. The 19th-century kasbah complex of Amerhidil on the right bank of the Oued Hajjaj, about 1km (½ mile) from the main road, is particularly fine, although it is slowly falling into ruin; as is the case with so many of these family castles, the owners have moved away.

Although the tamarisks lining the entry into the town by the El-Mansour Eddahbi reservoir look a promising start, **Ouarzazate** (pop. 40,000), 311km (193 miles), is rather disappointing, being nothing but a modern town with a famous kasbah. It also has its origins in a French garrison, built to the west of the clay-walled village of Taourirt with its gigantic ★★ **Glaoui Kasbah**. This is one of the largest and most impressive of the feudal castles of the Glaoua clan, whose famous leader, Thami-el-Glaoui, ruled over a large part of southern Morocco during the time of the French protectorate (*see page 13*). It has been partly restored by the state and some of the ceremonial rooms are open to the public. The culture and congress centre, a film studio and a golf course, that have been established here at some expense, reveal which section of society patronises Ouarzazate. The Royal Golf Course is situated by the reservoir, and dates from the early 1990s. The clubhouse in kasbah style stands on the shore of the lake, where the super-rich of this world also have their luxurious holiday villas.

With the surrounding Atlas scenery being so similar to Tibet, the film studios to the north of the town centre are popular among producers of 'Tibet' movies, including Martin Scorcese's film, *Kundun*, released in 1998.

Route 15

From the coast to the desert

Casablanca – Marrakech – Tizi-n-Tichka – Ouarzazate – Agdz – Zagora (605km/376 miles)

Marrakech with its Jemaa el-Fna Square, its mosques, medina and many other attractions is the principal city and one of the major highlights of this route. However, on the way there and between Marrakech and Zagora, there are many unusual sights on either side of the 4,000-m (13,000-ft) peaks of the High Atlas, such as the three best-known kasbahs: Dar Glaoui, Aït-Benhaddou and Taourirt. Ouarzazate is a useful halfway stage along

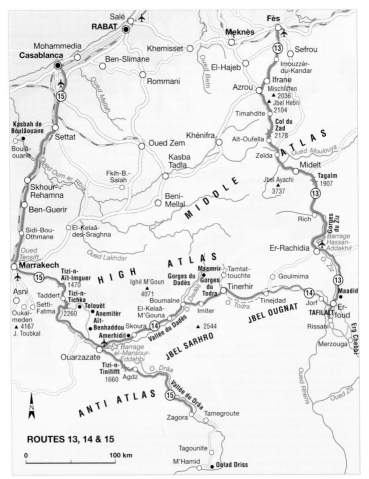

ROUTES 13, 14 & 15

0   100 km

this route to the desert. Another fascinating world opens out in the Vallée du Draâ. Allow at least three days for this route.

As essential as the fertile Chaouïa alluvial plain and the phosphate are to the country's economy, from a tourist point of view the stretch between Casablanca (*see pages 22–25*) and Marrakech is rather monotonous.

Of the towns en route, only **Settat** (pop. 96,200) is of interest. The administrative centre of the rising province of the same name is described as Morocco's granary. The modern agricultural centre, which has also become an industrial and university town, is now anxious to profit from expanding tourism.

A detour (50km/31 miles each way) can be made from Settat to the **Kasbah de Boulâouane**. The road runs through wooded countryside and finally crosses the river Oum er Rbia. The kasbah with its mosque was built by Moulay Ismaïl in the year 1710, and stands on a hill; from the battlements and the minaret there is a splendid view of the fertile valley with the river winding through it.

The outlook from the Kasbah de Boulâouane

After Sidi-Bou-Othmane, the main road passes through the Jbilet hills, and soon the Koutabia minaret of Marrakech (*see pages 38–43*) comes into view (237km/147km).

On the second stage of this route, the road through the Atlas from Marrakech to Ouarzazate is initially lined with eucalyptus and tamarisks and luxuriant olive groves on either side. It crosses small tributaries of the Oued Tensift such as the Oued R'Mat and Oued Zate on the way to the first pass in the High Atlas, **Tizi-n-Aït-Imguer** (1,470m/4,823ft). Olive trees give way to holm oaks, and tiny villages with small houses built of rough red stone or clay cling to the slopes. **Taddert** on the Rdat torrent is already at a height of 1,650m (5,413ft), and is surrounded by walnut trees. The extent to which tourism has invaded this area is demonstrated by the number of teenagers trying to interest travellers in Atlas stones (amethyst, onyx) of varying quality. They are sold too from shops and stalls on the ★ **Tizi-n-Tichka**. At a height of 2,260m (7,415ft), there is usually a biting wind on this pass, which is surrounded by a wilderness of steep, bare, yellowish slopes.

Vendor near the Tizi-n-Tichka

On the other side of the pass, a narrow road on the left leads eastwards for 21km (13 miles) to the community of **Teloùet** at the heart of the southern tribal area of the Glaoua Berbers. This powerful tribe once ruled over the entire region southeast of Marrakech and from the early

Telouèt from the kasbah

Anemitèr

Aït-Benhaddou: kasbah detail

19th century controlled important pass roads used by the trans-Atlas traffic. Here, at a height of 1,800m (5,096ft), surrounded by furrowed red 3,000-m (10,000-ft) peaks, is the ★★ **Dar Glaoui Kasbah**, the former main residence of the Glaoui *caïds*. A watchman guides you through the massive complex, which was built in several stages from the mid-19th century onwards. It is not only the size of the kasbah that is impressive, but also the Moorish decoration of the reception rooms in the most recent tract, although unfortunately most of the complex is now falling into ruin. The Glaoua souk takes place on Thursdays.

The road descends for another 13km (8 miles) to the delightful village of ★ **Anemitèr**, located in a broad green valley on the old caravan route between Aït-Benhaddou and Telouèt. Some guidebooks (and maps) suggest that from here it is easy to continue the journey south for 45km (28 miles) to Aït-Benhaddou. This, however, is not advised except, perhaps, to very experienced four-wheel drivers. Immediately after the village, the road degenerates into a narrow track, extremely bumpy and often accompanied by frightening drops to the valley below. Water courses also have to be negotiated. It is much safer to return to the main road via Telouèt and approach Aït-Benhaddou from the south, along a road which forks off to the north of Ouarzazate.

Set on a steep hillside, the fortified village of ★★★ **Aït-Benhaddou**, consisting of a complex of kasbahs, has long been a popular destination and has also been the location of many big films, including Robert Aldrich's 1963 *Sodom and Gomorrah*, starring Stewart Granger, and Martin Scorsese's controversial *Last Temptation of Christ* (1988): these almost deserted kasbahs, some of which have been faithfully restored by UNESCO, look just like stage sets. Local guides will show you around, but it is also possible to walk around at leisure, perhaps ascending through the maze of alleys and then onwards and upwards until you reach the lookout tower at the top of the hill. Souvenir stalls line the track connecting the modern centre with old Aït-Benhaddou.

After this detour, continue along the main road to Ouarzazate (*see page 75*).

After a last glimpse of Ouarzazate against the backdrop of the High Atlas, the road climbs through the forbidding stony deserts of the Jbel Tifernine to its high point of the Tiz-n-Tinififft (1,660m/5,466ft). To the east the 2,500-m (8,000-ft) pinnacles of the rugged Jbel Sarho rise above the haze; to the south the road spirals down to the oasis of **Agdz** and the first date palms of the fabled ★★★ **Vallée du Drâa** come into view.

Tamenougalt in the Drâa Valley

There are date-palm oases, interspersed with the towers of numerous *ksour* and kasbahs, all along the winding course of the Drâa. Five kilometres (3 miles) southeast of Agdz, notice beyond the left bank of the river the old *ksar* of **Tamenougalt** with its amazing defensive architecture. Further south, the village of **Tinezouline** is the scene of a colourful market held on Mondays and Thursdays. Here you are likely to come across large numbers of dark-skinned people, whose ancestors were brought to this part of southern Morocco as slaves from the Sudan.

Zagora (pop. 26,000), 605km (376 miles), is the main market of the south. Nomadic Ait Atta, Saharan Berbers who found their way into Morocco in the 17th century, mix with old Arab families who emigrated from the Arabian peninsula eight centuries ago. Camel caravans from the south used to break their journeys here before continuing onwards north and east. A sign saying 'Timbouctou 52 jours' is a reminder of the days of the trade caravans.

Zagora's main street is lined with souvenir shops and restaurants, and there is a goodly number of hotels. The town is the starting point for expeditions to the edge of the desert: it is another 18km (11 miles) from here to the oasis of **Tamegroute**, which has an interesting library in the Zaouïa Sidi M'Hami Ben Nacer and a pottery.

From Tamegroute it is another 79km (50 miles) across mostly barren but beautiful terrain to **M'Hamid**. There is a souk every Monday, where dromedaries may also be seen. Also in M'Hamid, young boys offer their services as guides into the surrounding desert, which is mostly stony but occasionally punctuated by impressive sand dunes. Camel safaris are the order of the day here, though it is also possible to negotiate the desert tracks in your hired Peugeot 205, known hereabouts as the 'Desert Scorpion'.

79

On route to Timbouctou

Architecture and Design

Side by Side

Here the old city, there the new city – wherever you travel in Morocco, all towns and cities are made up of two totally contrasting parts. Until the start of the protectorate, all Moroccan cities were just medieval walled medinas (medina = city). The colonial powers left these medinas alone, choosing instead to house their administration and settlers in new towns – Villes Nouvelles – outside the walls, built in elegant colonial style. There was, after all, enough room in this thinly populated country and the way of life of the medinas had to be respected. The French left space between the medina and the new town by establishing green belts or situating the new town on the opposite side of the river.

Opposite: tiled fountain in Fès

After the withdrawal of the colonial powers, the richer and most influential families moved out of the confines of the medinas into the more modern quarters vacated by the Europeans, leaving the medinas to the powerless and populous poor. At the same time, migrants from the countryside came to settle in the medinas, causing severe overcrowding. These demographic, social and economic constraints have led to a severe deterioration in the fabric of the medinas. Programmes involving restoration and rehousing have been introduced to alleviate the situation, notably in Fès, but it is a mammouth task.

However decrepit a town house exterior may be, visitors to the medinas will often be surprised by what lies behind the walls. Perhaps taken over by a restaurant or carpet business, many of the interiors are stunningly beautiful.

The old and the new in Fès

Berber architecture

One of the most fascinating forms of settlement in Morocco is the *ksar* (pl. *ksour*), a fortified village often only inhabited by a single clan, ethnic or social group. A *ksar* usually consists of two- to three-storey houses built closely together, open or covered mud alleys, a mosque, a *hammam* and storage rooms. The whole complex was originally protected by a wall, and the gate kept shut at night. Today, the rather neglected *ksour* are administered from modern centres, equipped with administrative buildings, a modern infrastructure and a space for the weekly souk. Each centre administers a certain number of surrounding *ksour* and usually bears the name of the largest and most important fortified village. The designers of the centres have occasionally integrated traditional architectural elements at least into the facades.

Simpler motifs south of the Atlas

Within the *ksour* there is often a kasbah, a separately fortified building with four corner towers built either to accommodate garrisons or for an important family. Most

Kasbah of Amerhidil, Skoura

The Bab Mansour
in Meknès, detail

kasbahs are isolated buildings in prominent positions, and several together form a kasbah complex. The upper part of the tapering towers and facades was frequently decorated with brick patterns.

The first fortified settlements were probably built between the 2nd and 4th centuries, and mainly developed in the areas traversed by the Saharan nomads. The caravan trade with black Africa brought prosperity both to the nomads and the settlers of the oases. People and animals were secure from robbery behind the fortified walls of their densely built clay-brick villages. The fortified villages and castles are still a dominant feature of the landscape from the High Atlas down to the edge of the Sahara, following one another in close succession along the high valleys of the desert rivers Ziz, Rheris, Todra, Dadès and Draâ. It is hence not without reason that the stretch of country from Ouarzazate to Er-Rachidia is advertised to tourists as the 'Road of the Kasbahs'.

Of the remaining kasbahs, the oldest date back around 300 years. Very few kasbahs are still inhabited, as the earth bricks weather very quickly and need constant maintenance. The fact that these clay castles still exist at all is due to the lack of rain in the south of Morocco. Unfortunately many of the deserted kasbahs are falling into ruin.

Moorish architecture

In Arab-occupied Spain between the 9th and 15th centuries, a new style of Islamic architecture developed which came to be known as the Hispano-Moorish style. Under the Almoravids and the Almohads it spread to Morocco and reached perfection with the Merinid sultans. The purest form of the Moorish style found expression in sacred buildings, mosques, medersas and mausoleums. There was a different form for the rulers' palaces, and the houses of the nobility and reception halls in the kasbahs of famous tribal leaders were built and decorated in only a slightly less lavish version of this.

Characteristic of this style are the saddle and pyramid roofs and canopies with their green-glazed tiles. Behind almost completely plain facades are rectangular courtyards surrounded by arcades, with double doors opening into narrow rooms. The classic form of decoration in this part of the building consists of tile mosaics in many different patterns. The walls are decorated with arabesques cut in the plaster and calligraphic Koran sura friezes and there are carved wooden ceilings painted in muted colours.

Today King Hassan is enthusiastically promoting a revival of this cultural heritage. There has been a genuine architectural renaissance with the building of costly sacral buildings such as the Mausolée de Mohammed V in Rabat and the Grande Mosquée d'Hassan II in Casablanca.

Arts and Crafts

On a walk through the souks it is the assortment of crafts that catches your eye. Colourful carpets, carved items of furniture and shining brass plates with filigree decoration all bear the hallmarks of tradition and craftsmanship. Arts and crafts are subsidised by the state, whether through the establishment of teaching workshops or the creation of co-operatives monitoring the quality and price. Craft products are also often used as decoration in hotels, the expression of a proud consciousness of tradition.

Traditional household objects and ornaments are in demand not just for Moroccan homes, but also for export. Objects such as teapots, wooden grilles or occasional tables marked *fabriqué au Maroc* (made in Morocco) are not only useful, but display a highly developed instinct for fine detail. The wide range of decorative elements in the craftwork of the rural regions is based on Berber tradition, with characteristic geometric and symbolic motifs. Warm, natural colours are used.

Fès, Safi, Marrakech, Salé and Tetouan are pottery centres. Hand-painted couscous and *harira* bowls are very common, as well as *tagines*, shallow, round bowls with conical lids for the traditional dishes of the same name.

Cedar, thuja, oak, walnut, acacia, lemon tree and ebony wood is the raw material used for the sophisticated carving work, which is centred for example in Azrou, Essaouira, Fès, Marrakech, Meknès, Rabat and Tetouan. Copper and brass articles, such as perforated hanging lamps, chased plates, candlesticks and incense burners, continue to be very popular. In demand, but not very cheap, are the individually made pieces of genuine Berber jewellery. There is a wide variety of clasps, earrings, bracelets and ornamental weapons made of silver, sold primarily in the southern part of the country.

Leather goods from Morocco are famous all over the world. Frequently however the goods, in particular the articles sold in the bazaars, do not come up to European standards. The best place to buy objects of good quality is in the craft centres in Marrakech and Fès. The colourful *babouches* (slipper-like shoes) that are sold everywhere make practical, inexpensive and popular presents.

And who is not familiar with the beautiful Berber and Oriental carpets which come from the Middle and High Atlas, Rabat and Mediouna. Each region produces its own type and specialises in particular motifs.

The hand-woven white, brown or striped materials, made of pure wool, are also very attractive. It is from these that the men have their winter *jellabas* (long, loose, hooded garment) made. The hand-made, but expensive kaftan worn by women on special occasions is very flattering.

Newly dyed wool

83

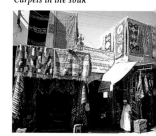
Carpets in the souk

Leather has many uses

On the way to the moussem

Festivals and Events

In addition to the national holidays, where there are parades and processions, and the religious holidays, which are based on the Islamic moon calendar, there are national and regional festivals that are worth experiencing.

Moussems, celebrations in honour of national and local holy figures – rulers, leaders of sects and miracle-workers – are legion. Lasting three to seven days and taking place in a series of tents put up for the occasion, they begin with prayers and sacrifices, and continue with *fantasias* (circus events with music and dancing that culminate in horseback feats on thoroughbred Arab and Berber horses) and firework displays.

You can find out when an event is on shortly beforehand in the tourist office of the place concerned. Sometimes, however, even annual festivals are cancelled or postponed at short notice.

Water-seller in attendance

May

Fête des Roses in El-Kelaâ M'Gouna (northeast of Ouarzazate) with a procession, election of the rose queen, folk dances and an arts and crafts exhibition.

May/June

Festival des Musiques Sacrées du Monde in Fès. Internationally known musicians and orchestras of the three monotheistic religions (Judaism, Christianity, Islam) gather here for a music festival.

June

Festival International de Musique Classique in Ouarzazate with visiting foreign symphony orchestras.

Fête des Cerises in Sefrou (33km/21 miles southeast of Fès). Cherry festival with folk dances and election of the cherry queen.

Festival National des Arts Populaires in Marrakech. The most important folklore festival in the country. Numerous dance troupes and musicians perform in the flood-lit ruins of the Palais d'el Badi.

August
Festival Culturel in Asilah (south of Tangier). International culture weeks with exhibitions, film shows, lectures and concerts.

The **Moussem de Moulay Abdallah Amghar**, an annual festival in honour of the great saint, is held in the coastal town of the same name south of El-Jadida. A huge complex of tents is constructed specially for this *moussem*, which features horseback events (*fantasias*), falconry and folk dances.

Falconry at the Moussem de Moulay Abdallah Amghar

September
In the remote mountains near Imilchil (province of Er-Rachidia, 130km/81 miles west of Rich) the **Moussem des Fiançailles** is held. On a plateau 2,000m (6,600ft) up, the Aït-Haddidou Berbers hold an annual festival in honour of their tribal holy man. It is also traditionally the occasion of numerous weddings, hence the name 'Wedding Moussem'. Folk dances, *fantasias*, a big fair and cattle market, overnight accommodation in tents.

Festival food

October
The time of the **date festivals** (fêtes des dattes) in the Tafi-lalt oases at Erfoud. Folk dances, date souks and the election of the date queen are on the programme.

December
Festival des Arts Populaires de la Région Sud with folk dances and many other events in Agadir.

Religious holidays
1 Moharrem: Beginning of the Islamic year. One day.
10 Moharrem: Achoura festival (festival of the 10th day). Children are given presents and celebrate. One day.
Aïd el-Maoulid: Birthday of the Prophet Mohammed. Two days.
Aïd el-Fitr: Fast-breaking festival, also known as the Aïd es-Seghir (little festival). This is the first day after the end of the fasting month of Ramadan. Two days.
Aïd el-Adha: Sacrificial festival, also known as Aïd-el-kebir (big festival). The high-point is the ritual slaughtering of a sacrificial ram in memory of the sacrifice of Abraham. Two days.

Snake charmer

Food and drink

In Morocco the tradition of hospitality in one's own home goes back centuries, and has worked against the establishment of a restaurant culture such as that in Europe. Although businessmen do meet in restaurants, this is still rather the exception. During the protectorate the French and the Spanish opened the first restaurants, which explains why in the Villes Nouvelles the restaurants mainly offer international cuisine, and at the most the menu will also include a *tagine*. In the meantime there are Italians offering pizza and pasta and Asian chefs bidding for custom with Far Eastern delicacies; the fast-food invasion has also reached the large towns.

At the market in Essaouira

Tagine and thé à la menthe

With the immigration of Muslim Arabs, new spices and unknown vegetables and ways of preparing them were introduced into the Moroccan cuisine. The traditional plain fare of the Berbers, nutritious dishes consisting of wheat, barley, semolina or simple, round flat loaves and braised or fried mutton suddenly became tastier and more varied with the addition of the new ingredients.

87

From the wide range of dishes only a few of the standard ones found on the menus of almost all restaurants are mentioned here.

Starters include *harira*, a soup made of pulses and cubes of meat and thickened with rice, *briouats*, stuffed puff pastry squares and *kbab*, lamb on skewers.

The tasty *tajine*, in all its variations, is served throughout the country. This main meal consists of a wide variety of vegetables according to season, which are stewed for hours with chicken, lamb or fish in a special earthenware bowl, and served piping hot.

Tajine pots

Couscous, the national dish and traditional Friday meal, consists of semolina which is steamed in a pan. Prepared with chicken, pigeon, lamb or veal and seasonal vegetables, it is a real delicacy.

No festive meal is complete without *pastilla*. This takes hours to prepare and consists of around 40 layers of very thin pastry (*warkha*), filled with almond paste and pigeon meat and sprinkled with castor sugar.

Mint tea for two

At the conclusion of a meal it is traditional to drink *thé à la menthe*. This hot, very sweet national drink is brewed from fresh mint and green tea, and is served with almond and honey biscuits. The mineral water in Morocco is of excellent quality. Wine and beer can only be sold by bars and restaurants with the corresponding licence.

The hotels usually provide both traditional and international fare. In restaurants the labels '*marocain*' and 'international' make the origin of the dishes clear.

In the medinas of Marrakech and Fès numerous old palaces have been turned into luxury restaurants. The Moorish atmosphere and exquisite dishes introduce customers to the magnificent lifestyle of the wealthy middle classes. Costumed waiters serve *pastilla*, *couscous* and *tagine* at low, round tables, and the finishing touch is provided by the strains of classical Andalusian music, Oriental belly-dancing or the tambourines of Berber folk musicians.

In towns such as Agadir, Marrakech, Ouarzazate and in some of the oases, restaurants also serve their guests in tents. The *caïd* tent, laid out with carpets, is a traditional part of Moroccan life, and is erected for *moussems*, weddings, and even royal visits.

Lunch time

Restaurant selection

Rabat
La Caravelle, in the Oudaïa Kasbah, tel: 733876. Fish restaurant on the terrace of the Portuguese fortress with a view of the beaches. $$. **La Clef**, corner of Rue Hatim and Av. Moulay Youssef, near the station, tel: 701972. French-Moroccan cuisine served on a shady terrace. $.

Succulent sausages in Meknès

Casablanca
Le Petit Poucet, 86 Boulevard Mohammed V, tel: 275420. French novelist Saint-Exupéry has been among its customers. $$. **Le Port de PIche**, by the fishing port, tel: 318561. Relaxed atmosphere with delicious fish dishes on the menu. $$. **Al Mounia**, 95 Rue du Prince Moulay Abdallah, east of the Place Mohammed V, tel: 222669. Well-known for its excellent Moroccan cuisine. $$$.

Meknès
Le Dauphin, 5 Av. Mohammed V, tel: 523432. Quiet atmosphere, fish is the best-seller. Closed Aïd el-Adha and Aïd el-Fitr. $$. **Zitouna**, 44 Jemaa Zitouna, by the Parc Zoologique el-Haboul, Bab Tizimi, medina, tel: 530281. Old Moorish house with serving personnel in costume. Also open during Ramadan. $$. **La Coupole**, corner of Av. Hassan II and Rue Ghana, tel: 522483. Founded in 1927. Moroccan and international menu. $.

Dates from the desert

Fès
La Maison Bleue, 2 Place de l'Istiqlal Batha in the medina, tel: 741843. In an old palace. Dine to music by Gnaoua musicians, excellent cuisine. $$$. **La Koubba du ciel**, in the Hotel Merinides, Borj Nord, tel: 646040. Under the 'heavenly dome' there is a panoramic view of Fès el-Bali. Moroccan and European cuisine. $$. **Oued de la Bière**, Bvd Mohammed V, by the Grand Hotel, tel: 651657. Simple bistro for a quick lunch with beer. $.

Harvest from the sea

Marrakech

Dar Marjana 15, Derb Sisi Ali Tair, tel: 445773. In a beautiful palace where the owner receives the guests himself. The full menu and drinks, to the accompaniment of Gnaoua music, is by no means cheap, but is an unforgettable experience. $$$. **Le Stylia**, 34 Rue Ksour, tel: 443587. Cosmopolitan meeting place of connoisseurs of Moroccan cuisine in a splendid Moorish setting. Closed in August. $$$. **Boule de Neige**, Place Abdelmoumen, 30 Rue Yougoslavie, Guéliz, tel: 435219. For all those tired of the usual hotel breakfast or who want to indulge in cakes and ice cream. In the pâtisserie you can buy sweet specialities to take away. $$. **Bagatelle**, 101 Rue Yougoslavie, tel: 430274. Solid homely French cuisine. $.

Tangier

Guitta's, 110 Rue Sidi Bouabid, tel: 937333. Here the cosmopolitan elite of the city sits down at tastefully decorated tables. $$$. **Romero**, 12 Av. Prince Moulay Abdellah, tel: 932277. Delicious paella; fish and seafood always served fresh from the sea. $$.

Essaouira

Chez Sam, Port de Pêche, tel: (04) 473513. Charming restaurant at the far end of the fishing port with a reputation for good fish cuisine. $$.

Safi

Le Refuge, 4km (2.5 miles) north on the El-Jadida road, tel: 464354. Fish cuisine and a view of the sea. $$

Oualidia

Parc à huitres Nr. 7 and **A l'Araignée Gourmande**, the motel restaurant, tel: (03) 346447, both restaurants specialise in oysters. $$.

'Come this way'

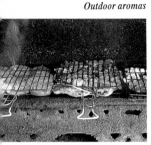
Outdoor aromas

El-Jadida
La Marquise, Bvd Mohammed V, tel: 342466. Fish and seafood. $$.

Agadir
Darkoum, Av. du Général Kettani, tel: 840622. Moroccan food with Oriental music and belly-dancing. $$$.
L'Amiral, Port de Pêche, tel: 846080. Owned by a former sailor, with fish straight from the sea on the menu. $$.

Tafraoute
L'Etoile du Sud, tel: 800038. The speciality is *tajines* with almonds, and there is also a *caïd* tent. $.

Tetouan
Palace Bouhlal, 48 Jamaa Kbir, tel: 974419. *Tajines* are served under round Moorish arches. $$.

Tea to finish

Chechaouèn
Tissemlal, 22 Rue Targui, tel: 986153. Good regional cuisine. $$.

90

Al-Hoceima
Karim, by the fishing harbour, tel: 982318. Fish straight from the sea all the year round. $.

Erfoud
Café-Restaurant la Jeunesse, 9 Av. Moulay Ismaïl. Simple restaurant with tasty Moroccan cuisine. $

Ouarzazate
La Kasbah, Av. Mohammed V, tel: 882033. Attractive terrace restaurant opposite the kasbah. Good Moroccan cuisine. $$.

Fresh figs

Active holidays

Mountain and desert

Mountaineers in particular will find a great deal to interest them in this country with its bizarre mountain scenery and remote villages. There are around 10 summits in the High Atlas over 4,000m (13,000ft) high, and many over 3,000m (10,000ft). Volcanic ranges such as the Jbel Siroua and the Jbel Sarhro are also well worth exploring.

Climbing in the Atlas

Trekking tours are led by mountain guides (*accompagnateurs de montagne brevetés*), trained in the French Alps and the High Atlas. Porters and mules carry the luggage and the participants sleep in huts, basic tourist accommodation, the homes of local people or tents.

The hikers experience a strange mountain world, with rock drawings from the Stone Age and earth-coloured Berber villages in green valleys, and meet the tradition-conscious mountain-dwellers. In the evenings there is *tagine* and *thé à la menthe* to the accompaniment of *bendir* (tambourine) music played by the muleteers.

Popular departure points for mountain adventures are Asni and Imlil south of Marrakech, where arrangements can usually be made on the spot for ascents of the country's highest mountain, Mt Toubkal. Travel companies are also expanding into more adventurous activities, such as mountain biking and white-water rafting (spring only for the latter). Camel trekking is increasingly popular in the desert dunes of the south, with excursions offered from Zagora and M'Hamid.

91

Biking down the Vallée Du Draâ

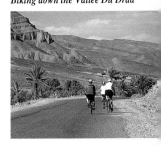

The Middle Atlas with the 2,036-m (6,680-ft) high Mischliffen, south of Ifrane, and the High Atlas with the 2,650-m (8,694-ft) Oukaïmeden plateau, south of Marrakech, are an El Dorado for winter sports fans.

Further information on camel trekking, climbing, ski-tours and mountain-bike tours can be obtained from: Ribat Tours, 3 Av. Moulay Youssef, Rabat, tel: (07) 700395 fax: 707535. Arabic, French and English are spoken.

Golf

King Hassan is a very enthusiastic golfer, and has ensured that his country is well provided with golf courses, including some of the best in the world. Several national and international tournaments take place under his patronage, including the prestigious Moroccan Open. There are currently 15 courses (Agadir, Ben-Slimane, Cabo-Negro, Casablanca, El-Jadida, Fès, Marrakech, Meknès, Mohammedia, Ouarzazate, Rabat, Settat, Tangier) and another 18 are planned by the year 2005.

Further information may be obtained from: Fédération Royale Marocaine de Golf, Royal Golf Dar Es-Salam, Rabat, tel: (07) 755960, fax: 751026

Getting There

Opposite: switchbacks at the head of the Gorges du Dadès

By air

Morocco's national airline, Royal Air Maroc (RAM), flies from London Heathrow and most of Europe's other principal cities to Tangier, Casablanca, Marrakech and Agadir. Some of the flights to Casablanca, Marrakech and Agadir involve a stop in Tangier. There are onward flights to Fès, Ouarzazate and other cities from Casablanca (*see page 94*). RAM direct flights to Casablanca also operate from New York, though not on a daily basis. For further information, contact Royal Air Maroc:

In the UK: 205 Regent Street, London W1, tel: 0171-439 4361.

In the US: 55 East 59th Street, Suite 17B, New York 10003, tel: 212-750 5115.

British Airways has linked up with GB Airways to run daily flights from London Gatwick to Casablanca (stopping in Gibraltar), as well as less frequent flights to Marrakech and Tangier. There are also flights to Essaouira.

Most airports connect to the nearest city by taxi, but Casablanca Airport now also has direct rail links with Casablanca, Rabat and Fès.

By rail

From Paris (Gare d'Austerlitz) there is a daily rail service with sleeping cars and couchettes to Madrid, where you change onto the train for Algeciras where you catch the ferry to Morocco (*see below*). The complete journey will take up to two days. Morocco participates in the Inter Rail scheme for young travellers.

By car

From Algeciras there are ferries several times a day to Tangier (2½ hours) and Spanish Ceuta (1¼ hours) and in July and August a shuttle service is run to cope with the extra traffic as many Moroccan emigrants go back to their own country for their holidays. There are also daily ferry connections from Malaga and Almeria to Spanish Melilla. A boat goes twice a week from Sète (South of France) to Tangier (36 hours) and in the summer there is also a ferry from Sète to Nador (36 hours).

Generally, travelling to Morocco by car is expensive (allow for toll fees in France and Spain as well as ferries and accommodation). For travel through France you will need Green Card Insurance, and for Spain a bail bond, both issued by your car insurers. For insurance in Morocco, it is best to make arrangements when you arrive. An international driving licence is not necessary in Morocco. If you want to take a caravan or trailer, consult the Moroccan Tourist Office for advice on necessary documents.

93

On the move

Negotiating the Todra

Bound for the desert

Getting Around

By air

Royal Air Maroc (RAM) and Royal Air Inter, operating from Casablanca, have flights to Agadir, Al-Hoceima, Dakhla, Er-Rachidia, Fès, Marrakech, Ouarzazate, Oujda, Rabat, Tangier and Tetouan. For contact details in the UK and US, *see page 93*.

Second-class carriage

By rail

Morocco's railway (ONCF) operates an approximately hourly service with air-conditioned fast trains (TNR = Trains Navette Rapides) connecting Casablanca, Rabat and Kénitra and between Casablanca and the Mohammed V Airport. Other rail connections between large towns are Casablanca–Rabat–Meknès–Fès–Oujda and Tangier–Asilah–Rabat–Casablanca–Marrakech.

From Marrakech the state railway company runs bus services to Agadir and into the Western Sahara as far as Dakhla.

By bus

Since most people do not have their own cars, the buses are the most inexpensive and frequently used means of transportation, particularly in the remoter areas. The safest and most comfortable way of travelling is with the privatised Compagnie de Transports au Maroc, abbreviated to CTM, which operates air-conditioned coaches that serve drinks and sometimes run films (CTM stations are often separate from the main bus station.) There are other private lines on the well-developed network of routes; in the south the best line is SATAS.

A differentiation is made between an autocar, a long-distance bus, and an autobus, which is a municipal bus.

By taxi

There are three types of taxi: *grand taxi*, *petit taxi* and *taxi collectif*. The expensive large taxis, most of them Mercedes, go everywhere, whereas the small taxis are only allowed to operate within municipal boundaries. They stop when waved down and are a different colour in every town. The cheap collective taxis complete the network of long-distance buses or run on subsidiary routes (e.g. between Rabat and Salé). There are fixed rates and the taxi does not set off until all six places are filled or paid for.

Option for about town

Hire cars

Well-maintained hire cars are only to be obtained from internationally known agencies, which are represented in large towns or at the airports. The driver must be at least 21 and have a national driving licence. Most car hire firms require a deposit. It is easier and often cheaper to hire in advance of arrival in Morocco. Four-wheel drive vehicles can only be hired with a driver.

Pit stop for a Peugeot

Traffic regulations

Whether the car is your own or hired, always keep the documents – licence and log book – handy to show gendarmes (traffic police), who stop motorists frequently, especially at major junctions or on the outskirts of towns. Infringement of the law – speeding etc – can mean an on-the-spot fine. Speed limits are 50kph (30mph) in urban areas, 100kph (60mph) on the open road and 120kph (74mph) on the motorway between Casablanca and Larache. The French system of *priorité à droite* (priority to the right) operates. This means that traffic engaged on a roundabout must give way to traffic coming on to the roundabout.

The road network is well developed and in good condition. However, many of the cross-country roads, particularly those south of the Atlas, do not always appear wide enough to accommodate your vehicle and the oncoming car, bus, lorry or fleet of four-wheel drives. In case of doubt, give oncoming vehicles enough room by pulling over onto the verge. You should try to avoid journeys at night, as unlit carts and bicycles, as well as careless pedestrians and animals, are frequently the cause of serious accidents.

Slow pace in Safi

Parking

Wherever you park in Morocco, there will be a *guardien* (parking attendant), though much of Casablanca now has parking meters. One or two dirhams is sufficient for a few hours, but overnight parking costs about 10 dirhams. Blatant infringement of parking regulations can result in the police attaching immobilising chains to the wheels or removing the number plate.

Facts for the Visitor

Travel documents

Your passport must be valid for at least another three months when you enter the country. British, Irish, Australian, Canadian, US and New Zealand passport holders do not require visas and are normally granted entry for 90 days.

'Can I help you?'

Tourist information

The Moroccan Tourist Board is well represented abroad, and provides helpful advice and assistance:

In the UK: 205 Regent Street, London W1R 7DE, tel: 0171-437 0073.

In the US: 20 East 46th Street, New York 10017, tel: 212-679 8635

In Morocco: Every major town or city has a Délégation du Tourisme. The main ones are: Rabat, 22 Av. d'Alger, tel:(07) 730562, fax: 727917; Casablanca, 55 Rue Omar Slaoui, tel: (02) 271177; Meknès, Place Administrative, tel: (05) 524426. Fès, Place de la Résistance, tel: (05) 623460, fax: 654370; Marrakech, Place Abdelmoumen Ben Ali, Guéliz, tel: (04) 436131, fax: 436057. Tangier, 29 Bvd Pasteur, tel: (09) 948661, fax: 948050; Agadir, Place du Prince Héritier Sidi Mohammed, Immeuble A, tel: (08) 846377, fax: 846378.

Currency and exchange

There are no restrictions on importing currency into the country. If you change all your money at the same bank or one of its branches, such as the Banque Marocaine du Commerce Exterieur (BMCE) or the Banque Populaire, you can change back dirhams at the same bank before you leave the country, for which you must keep all your currency exchange slips.

The dirham (DH) is divided into 100 centimes. There are 10, 20, 50, 100 and 200 DH notes and coins of 1, 5 and 10DH and of 5, 10, 20 and 50 centimes. Banks, leading hotels and shops accept Eurocheques and the major credit cards. In the large hotels, main stations and the centres of big cities there are currency exchange offices, which are open longer than the banks. The main cities also have ACMs (automatic cash machines).

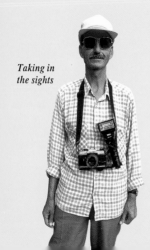

Taking in the sights

Customs

There is no restriction on items for personal use. The importing of radio equipment is forbidden and built-in radios in cars are confiscated. When reentering your own country, every person over 17 has a duty-free allowance of 200 cigarettes or 250g tobacco, 2 litres wine, 1 litre spirits. The import and export of Moroccan dirhams is forbidden.

Tipping
Leave 10 percent of the bill if you are satisfied with the service in a restaurant. Porters get 10 to 50DH.

Begging
There are still beggars on the streets of Morocco. In the main tourist centres travellers are pestered all the time. Acknowledged beggars such as the mentally ill and the old or crippled are accorded great respect in Islam and the giving of alms is written into the Koran.

Opening times
Shops in the Villes Nouvelles: Monday to Saturday 8am–12pm and 2.30–6.30pm, closed Sunday; the medinas have no fixed hours, and are usually closed Friday.
Banks: Monday to Thursday 8.15–11.30am and 2.15–4.30pm, Friday 8.15–11.15am and 2.45–4.45pm, Saturday and Sunday closed; during Ramadan banks are open continuously till the early afternoon.
Tourist and post offices: Monday to Thursday 8.30am–12pm and 2.30–6.30pm, Friday 8.30–11.30am and 3–6.30pm, Saturday and Sunday closed; during Ramadan open continuously till the early afternoon.

Colourful kaftans

Public holidays
1 January, 3 March (Feast of the Throne), 1 May, 23 May (referendum concerning the coming of age of the Crown Prince at 16), 9 July (birthday of Hassan II), 14 August (Allegiance Day: act of allegiance [*Baïa*] by the Sahraouis in Dakhla to Hassan II), 20 August (exile of Mohammed V), 21 August (birthday of Crown Prince Sidi Mohammed), 6 November (Marche Verte into the Western Sahara), 18 November (Independence Day).

The dates of religious holidays are determined by the Islamic moon calendar, which is 10 to 11 days shorter than the Gregorian calendar. The Islamic holidays are thus moveable (*see Culture, page 85*).

Postal services
Post offices are marked Poste, Télégraphe, Téléphone (PTT). Telephone boxes are to be found inside and in front of post offices, in stations and in front of cafés. For longer conversations it is worth buying a telephone card, obtainable in the post offices and at newspaper kiosks. Personally-attended tele-boutiques are also widespread.

Daily news

Newspapers
International newspapers are on sale at the newspaper stands and in the tobacco shops of the large towns and well-known holiday resorts such as Agadir. French newspapers predominate.

Undercover salesperson in Marrakech

Security

In general, Morocco is a safe country to travel in. However, in the press of the souks theft may occur, although this is not common. As a precaution, however, deposit your papers and valuables in the hotel safe or carry them concealed on your body.

On trips through the Rif Mountains stopping, even on open stretches, should be avoided at all costs: drug dealers will appear immediately and aggressively try to sell you hashish (*kif*). Sometimes cars with tourists are pursued and forced to halt: keep calm and make it absolutely clear you are not prepared to buy, but if you have no option, throw it out of the window later.

Clothing

Correct dress is important for Moroccans. The local people in the medinas and in the country are often offended by people wearing shorts.

Guides

In order to visit a medina undisturbed, an official guide is essential. These state-examined tourist guides can be obtained through the tourist office or the reception desk of the hotels. The tourist police (*brigade touristique*) is currently getting tough with *faux-guides* (fake guides), who are to be found outside all large hotels.

Time

Morocco keeps Greenwich Mean Time all year round.

Voltage

Electricity is 220 and 110V. It is advisable to take an adaptor with you.

Medical

No vaccinations are necessary for travellers from Europe. It is however recommended to drink only bottled mineral water. In the towns medical care is good. Addresses of doctors and dentists can be obtained at the reception desk of large hotels. It is advisable to take out a health insurance policy for travel abroad.

Connecting people

Emergencies

Police (Police secours): tel: 19
Ambulance (Ambulance): tel: 15.
Traffic police (Gendarmerie): tel: 177.

Diplomatic representation

UK: 17 Boulevard de la Tour Hassan, Rabat, tel: (07) 720905.
US: 2 Avenue de Marrakech, Rabat, tel: (07) 762265.

Accommodation

La Mamounia in Marrakech

99

Whether by the sea, in the cities or in the oases, by and large Morocco's hotel buildings blend harmoniously with their surroundings. Modern architects frequently use traditional style elements and incorporate decorative gateways, green courtyards or, in large hotel complexes, Andalusian gardens with tiled paths, marble fountains and pavilions with green-glazed pyramid roofs.

The selection below for some of the most popular centres is listed according to three categories: $$$ = expensive; $$ = moderate; $ = inexpensive.

Hotels in the main cities
Agadir
Medina Palace, Bvd du 20 Août, tel: 845353, fax: 845308. Extensive Moorish-style complex a few minutes from the beach. $$$. **Sahara**, Bvd Mohammed V, tel: 840660, fax: 840738. Attractive combination of modern and Moorish décor, with apartments and bungalows as well as hotel rooms. $$.

Casablanca
Safir, 160 Av. des F.A.R. (centre), tel: 311212, fax: 316 514. Caters for mixture of business travellers, yuppies and wealthy people. There is a selection of restaurants and the hotel has its own nightclub. $$$. **Hyatt Regency**, Place. Mohammed V, tel: 261234, fax: 220180. Right in the centre with a view over the city. The bar is the meeting place of the *jeunesse dorée*. $$$. **Les Almohades**, Av. Hassan I, tel. and fax: 220505. High-quality establishment for guests with high standards, with a stylish Moroccan restaurant. $$. **Moussafir**, Av. Bahamad/Place de la Gare, tel: 401984, fax: 400799. Modern hotel with Moorish-style courtyard close to the station. $$.

Luxury in Casablanca

Marrakech balcony

Welcome in Tangier

Fès

Jnan Palace, Av. Ahmed Chaouki, Ville Nouvelle, tel: 652230, fax: 651917. White building (1992) divided into wing sections, providing oriental luxury. $$$. **Palais Jamaï**, Bab Guissa, Fès el-Bali, tel: 634331, fax: 635096. Former 19th-century vizier palace with contemporary comfort. $$$. **Merinides**, Borj Nord, tel: 646040, fax: 645229. Splendid terrace high above Fès el-Bali. $$$. **Moussafir**, Av. des Almohads, tel: 651902, fax: 651909. This hotel is very close to the station. Garden, pool and good food. $$.

Marrakech

La Mamounia, Bab el-Jdid, tel: 448981, fax: 444660. Winston Churchill came to relax and paint in this super-luxurious hotel. The many other international prominent guests come not just to enjoy the winter sun in the 7-hectare (17-acre) Garden of Eden. $$$. **Palmeraie Golf Palace**, Circuit de la Palmeraie, tel: 301010, fax: 305050. Moorish-style El Dorado for golfers; pavilions with pyramid roofs, five swimming pools, restaurants, eight restaurants and golf course. $$$. **Tichka**, Semialia, tel: 448710, fax: 448691. American know-how and Moroccan creativity combine to make a paradise for tourists. $$. **Oasis**, Av. Mohammed V, tel: 447179, fax: 451088. Basic hotel, centrally located. $.

Meknès

Transatlantique, Rue El-Merineyne, tel: 525050, fax: 520057. Fine hotel with a view of the medina. In the large grounds a summer buffet is set out by the pool. $$$. **Zaki**, Bvd El-Massira, in the direction of El-Hajeb, tel: 514146, fax: 524836. Moorish interiors and a fine view of Ismaïl's city wall. The hotel has its own nightclub. $$. **Rif**, 10 Rue d'Accra, city centre, tel: 522591, fax: 524428. Quiet rooms facing the inner courtyard. $$.

Rabat

Rabat Hilton, Souissi, tel: 675656, fax: 671492. Not far from Chellah, it serves as the guesthouse of the royal palace. $$$. **Chellah**, 2, rue d'Infni, tel: 70101, fax: 706354. Large modern hotel. $$. **Balima**, Av. Mohammed V, tel: 708625, fax: 707450. Centrally located, traditional hotel. $$. **Royal**, 1 Rue Amman, tel: 721171, fax: 725491. Colonial-style hotel with a view over the Moulina mosque to the municipal park. $. **Splendid**, 24, Rue de Ghazza, tel: 723283. Centrally located. $.

Tangier

El Minzah, 85 Rue de la Liberté, city centre, tel: 935885, fax: 934546. The best hotel in Tangier famous for its reasonably priced restauarnt, just a short hop from the medina. It has its own nightclub. $$$. **Tanjah Flandria**, 6 Bvd Mohammed V, tel: 933279, fax: 934347. Recommended for those who prefer to do their sightseeing on foot. $$$.

Other selected hotels

Al-Hoceima

Quemado, by the beach, tel: 983315, fax: 983314. Rooms and bungalows in the best part of the bay with a panoramic view; only open in the summer. $$.

Asni

La Roseraie, tel: (04) 432094, fax: 432095. Rural-style chalets and a swimming pool surrounded by a rose garden. $$.

Boulmalne

El Madayeq, tel: (04) 830031, fax: 882223. High up with a splendid panoramic view. $$.

Boulmalne, view from El Madayeq

Chechaouene

Parador, Place Makhzen, tel: (09) 986324. Renovated colonial-era hotel with a lovely viewing terrace. $$.

El-Jadida

Palais Andalous, Bvd Docteur de Lanouy, tel: 343745. Former residence of a pacha. $$.

El-Kelaâ M'Gouna

Les Roses du Dadès, tel: (04) 836007. Situated on a terrance above the Asif M'Goun river, a tributary of the Dadès. Great views. $$.

Erfoud

Tafilalet, Av. Moulay Ismaïl, tel: (05) 576535, fax: 576036. The hotel lobby is like a giant desert tent. $$.

Doorway in Erfoud

Er-Rachidia

Rissani, on road to Erfoud, by the bridge over the Ziz, tel: 572186, fax: 572585. Attractive garden and swimming pool. $$.

Essaouira

Des Iles, Bvd Mohammed V, tel: (04) 472329, fax: 472472. Large hotel opposite the beach. $$. **Villa Maroc**, 10, Rue Abdellah Ben Yacine, tel: (04) 476147, fax: 475806. Exquisitely furnished rooms in two restored 18th-century houses in the heart of the medina. Friendly, intimate atmosphere, good cuisine. $$. **Tafouket**, Bvd Mohammed V, tel: (04) 472504, fax: 472416. Basic, clean hotel, rooms with a view of the sea. $.

Décor in Ouarzazate

Guelmim

Salam, Route de Tan-Tan, tel: (08) 872057. Situated near the souk in the Nouvelle Ville, this hotel also offers good food but is somewhat run down. $.

Kénitra

Safir, Place Administrative, tel: (07) 371921. Best hotel in town, with a swimming-pool. $$.

Merzouga

Les Dunes d'Or. A magical atmosphere, especially in the evening when local people from the oases come to play music. Basic, but clean rooms. $.

M'Hamid

Reda, on the road to M'Hamid, tel: (04) 847079, fax: 847012. Built in kasbah style on the banks of the Draâ. Several restaurants around the pool. $$.

Midelt

Kasbah Asma, 1km (½ mile) along the the road to Er-Rachidia, tel: (05) 583945. New hotel, flower garden. $$$.

Mohammedia

Miramar, Rue de Fès, tel: (03) 312443, fax: 324613. The best address in town. $$$. **Amphitrite**, tel: (07) 742220, fax: 742317. This hotel is by the beach of Skhirat. $$. **La Kasbah**, tel: (07) 749133, fax: 749116. By Ech-Chi-ahna beach. $$. **La Felouque**, tel: (07) 744559, fax: 744388. By Sables d'Or beach , on a side road. $$.

Moulay-Idriss

Hotel Volubilis, tel: (05) 544405, fax: 544369. This well-kept hotel with a panoramic view of the ruins of Volu-